PUPPET PROGRAMS
No. 6

15 Scripts Based on
New Testament Stories

by Doug Smee

Lillenas Publishing Company
Kansas City, MO 64141

Contents

Foreword

This is the page where many authors take time to indulge themselves with lofty words and noble thoughts. I will understand if you somehow manage to skip this page. However, I do want to thank some people. (1) My wife, Nancy, who has put up with my nights of writing and rewriting this and other books. Unfortunately, I do my best work around midnight. (2) My mother and father, Harriet and Don, from whom I have inherited my sense of humor, my work ethic, and my good teeth. (3) Last, but not least, the Lord Jesus who has given me the honor of serving Him and His children these past 15 years.

In His service,
DOUG

Up on the Rooftop

Biblical Text: Mark 2:1-12; Matthew 17:20

Scene Preparation: Place a large hardback book, like a dictionary, encyclopedia, or Bible, standing up on the table. Ask different children to come up and try to blow it down. Say, "Even when things seem impossible, don't give up. Have faith. There is always a way." Take a small paper bag and place it under the book. Have a child blow into the bag, and the book will fall over.

Cast: NARRATOR and PUPPET

NARRATOR: One of the fun things we get to do with our puppets is introduce you to people who knew Jesus. I can hardly wait to meet our character for today.

(Enter PUPPET.*)*

PUPPET *(mumbling):* Brittlebratten-razzelbrazzel, pooh!

NARRATOR *(to audience):* My, doesn't he sound like a cheerful fellow.

PUPPET: Well, what are you staring at?

NARRATOR: Sorry. We were waiting for someone else. Someone who knew Jesus and . . .

PUPPET: Jesus!?! You bet I know Jesus! If I never see Him again it will be too soon!

NARRATOR: Really? What's wrong?

PUPPET: I just got back from my insurance agent.

NARRATOR: I don't understand. What could Jesus and your insurance agent possibly have in common?

PUPPET: The hole in my roof.

NARRATOR *(shaking head):* You lost me. I can understand you wanting to talk to your insurance agent about the hole in your roof, but . . .

PUPPET: . . . But my vandalism insurance won't cover it!

NARRATOR: I'm sorry about that, but what does Jesus have to do with the hole?

PUPPET: He's the one who caused it.

NARRATOR: Why don't you start at the beginning.

PUPPET: OK. I was born in a little town outside of . . .

NARRATOR: No! I mean the beginning of the story about Jesus.

PUPPET: Oh, yeah. About a week ago I was talking to one of my good friends who knew this guy, Jesus.

NARRATOR: One of His disciples?

PUPPET: That's right. Anyway, he was saying how Jesus was always having to teach out in the desert, and wouldn't it be nice if He could come speak in the city sometime.

NARRATOR: Sounds good so far.

PUPPET: I thought so too. In fact, I realized that I could help out and maybe turn a little profit for myself.

NARRATOR (dryly): How thoughtful of you.

PUPPET: I know. I happen to have one of the biggest houses in Capernaum, and I offered it to be used, out of the goodness of my heart.

NARRATOR: . . . And a small fee.

PUPPET: Right.

NARRATOR: Did a good crowd show up?

PUPPET: I mean to tell you we packed them in. Everybody was there. We had people waiting all night in one spot just so they could see and hear Jesus.

NARRATOR: I'm surprised you weren't selling peanuts and popcorn. (PUPPET stares at NARRATOR for a few seconds.) Oh, no. You didn't. Peanuts and popcorn?

PUPPET: And Cracker Jacks. There's nothing wrong with turning a little profit.

NARRATOR: I can't say I like the sound of it. But, anyway, you had really packed them in, right?

PUPPET: Right. Inside and outside. Even space at one of the windows was going for a premium.

NARRATOR: Sounds like a great success.

PUPPET: It was, until those troublemakers came along.

NARRATOR: What troublemakers?

PUPPET: The ones who tore up my roof.

6

NARRATOR: Why would they do that?

PUPPET: I guess they couldn't get this sick friend of theirs through the crowd around the house. They spoiled the whole meeting for one little cripple.

NARRATOR: That doesn't sound like they wanted too much trouble.

PUPPET: Hey, these four dudes come up to my house carrying this other guy on a stretcher. Of course when they got closer, they couldn't get the people to move out of the way.

NARRATOR: It seems the people could have been more helpful.

PUPPET: Those people had been waiting a long time to see Jesus. Besides, these guys didn't have tickets or reservations.

NARRATOR *(sarcastically):* How thoughtless of them.

PUPPET: True. Anyway, when they couldn't even get to a door or a window, they climbed up on the roof and started ripping up my NEW IMPORTED ROMAN TILES.

NARRATOR: Steady, now. What happened next?

PUPPET: Well, then the four dudes lower the cripple right down into the middle of the room . . . right in front of Jesus.

NARRATOR: You must have been surprised.

PUPPET: Oh, really? *(Building in intensity)* Don't you think I expected to see my roof torn apart and a man lowered into my living room!

NARRATOR: My, you can get touchy, can't you. I suppose you really yelled at these people.

PUPPET: I was going to, but I thought Jesus would take care of that. After all, they had spoiled His talk, covered Him with dust, and embarrassed His gracious host, that's me.

NARRATOR: Did He yell at them?

PUPPET: No! You know what He did? He smiled at them. Smiled! I couldn't believe it!

NARRATOR: Well, all they wanted was for Jesus to heal their friend.

PUPPET: Then why couldn't He have done it quickly and gotten rid of the filthy beggar. But NO! He has to start a big argument among some very important people by saying the man's sins were forgiven. It seemed to last forever. I was so embarrassed.

NARRATOR: Did Jesus heal the man?

PUPPET: Oh, sure. Eventually.

NARRATOR: Well, that's terrific!

PUPPET: What's so terrific!?! Instead of a quiet meeting, my house is torn up, and we almost have a brawl between the religious leaders of our community. Then, to top it off, the house is overrun by everybody bringing in their sick friends and relatives. It was a disaster.

NARRATOR: I still think it's great that Jesus performed a miracle in your house. But I am sorry about your insurance. Why won't they pay for the damages?

PUPPET: Well, after I got through telling my agent the story, he said he couldn't call the damage vandalism.

NARRATOR: What did he call it?

PUPPET: An act of God.

(PUPPET *exits.*)

NARRATOR: I think he was right.

Focus Questions:

1. Why did the four friends need to climb up on the roof?
2. What did Jesus do first when the paralized man was placed before Him?
3. Why did Jesus first forgive the man's sins?
4. Do you think that was more important than making him walk? Why?
5. Do you have friends who would go to so much trouble to bring you to Jesus?
6. Do you care enough about someone to bring him to Jesus?

Jesus' Power and Protection

Biblical Text: Mark 4:35-41

Scene Preparation: Bring an older child up for an "experiment." Tell the child he must concentrate on the tip of your nose. Have him stand no more than a foot away from you. When he is concentrating, SCREAM! Ask the child how he feels. Talk to the kids. Say something like, "Everybody has been scared. When were you scared the most?" Take some responses. "What did it feel like?" Read the Bible story from Mark.

Cast: NARRATOR and PUPPET

NARRATOR: Do you know why we use our puppets so often to tell our stories? It's because they use their imaginations so well. Right now I need them to use their imaginations to tell our story. Come up here and help, please. I need your help.

(PUPPET *enters.*)

PUPPET: And what can I do for you?

NARRATOR: Well, I want to tell a story, but I need your help and imagination to tell it. Do you think you can do it?

PUPPET: Will I be the only person to use my imagination?

NARRATOR: No. Everyone will use theirs also. Can you help me?

PUPPET: But ... uh ... I don't know what the story is.

NARRATOR: That's OK. You don't need to know.

PUPPET: But I might make a booboo if I do not know the story.

NARRATOR: You would make booboos even if you knew what the story was about. This way you at least have an excuse.

PUPPET *(indignantly to the audience):* That is the way it is in show business. You get to top and everybody takes potshots at you.

NARRATOR: Are you ready?

PUPPET: OK. Let's get this over with.

NARRATOR: Cover your eyes.

PUPPET: Everyone else too.

NARRATOR: All right. We'll all do it.

PUPPET *(peeking):* Not everyone is covering his eyes.

NARRATOR: How would you know?

PUPPET *(covering eyes again):* Just guessing.

NARRATOR: I want you to imagine a big lake.

PUPPET: OK. A big lake. I see it coming! There it is! A big sparkling purple lake!

NARRATOR: Purple?!? Lakes aren't purple.

PUPPET: Mine is.

NARRATOR *(through teeth):* Lakes are not purple!

PUPPET *(uncovering eyes):* But purple is more interesting.

NARRATOR: Blue, please.

PUPPET: Yellow?

NARRATOR: Blue!

PUPPET: OK. There it is. A boring, blue lake.

NARRATOR: Believe me, this lake will not be boring. This big lake is called Galilee. I want you to imagine that you live by this lake and own a boat on it.

PUPPET: Oh boy! *(Moves to stage right, facing stage left)* Varrooom! Varrooom! Varrooom!

NARRATOR: Uh, I think we need to talk.

PUPPET *(to imaginary person):* Hit it, Charlie! Varrooom! Varroom! *(Exit stage left very rapidly)* Splash!

NARRATOR: What are you doing?

PUPPET: Water-skiing, sort of.

(Gets towel and dries self off)

NARRATOR: You are a *fisherman.* You own a sailboat, not a speedboat.

PUPPET: Gotcha. *(Exits and returns with a sailor's cap)* I'm ready.

NARRATOR *(shaking head):* If only I was. Anyway, your boat is going to be a special boat because Jesus is going to ride on it.

10

PUPPET: Right. Sounds good to me.

NARRATOR: Jesus has just finished a day of teaching and healing and is very tired.

PUPPET: Ahhh, maybe He can take a nap?

NARRATOR: Good idea! Jesus lays down in the back of the boat and goes to sleep while the boat rocks gently back and forth on the waves.

PUPPET *(rocking back and forth):* I think I'm going to like being a sailor.

NARRATOR: For a couple of hours you sail along into the night . . . but, look!

PUPPET *(turning around):* Where, where?!?

NARRATOR: There on the horizon! What is it?

PUPPET *(rocking back and forth):* How should I know? I just got here.

NARRATOR *(raising voice):* It's a group of gigantic storm clouds!

PUPPET *(raising voice to same level):* But they're moving away from us!

NARRATOR *(lowers voice, speaking specifically to* PUPPET): No, they're not.

PUPPET *(lowers voice, speaking specifically to* NARRATOR): Hey, whose imagination is this anyway?

NARRATOR *(raising voice again):* They're rushing toward you! The wind starts to whip the little sailboat about!

PUPPET *(rocking back and forth faster):* Help! Mommy! Help!

NARRATOR: Waves break over the little boat, thunder crashes, lightning flashes!

PUPPET *(rocking back and forth faster;* PUPPET *screams):* HELP!

NARRATOR: The little boat starts to sink!

PUPPET *(rocking back and forth):* Abandon ship! Man the lifeboats! Women and puppets first!

NARRATOR: You don't have any lifeboats!

PUPPET *(rocking back and forth):* Whose lousy ship is this anyway!?!

NARRATOR: Yours.

PUPPET *(rocking back and forth):* Oh. I don't suppose we could wade ashore?

NARRATOR: I'm afraid not. Are you scared?

PUPPET *(rocking back and forth):* Try terrified! I don't swim. And it is very hard to breathe under water. Clogs up the sinuses, you know.

NARRATOR: Well, don't forget you have Jesus on board.

PUPPET *(rocking back and forth):* That's right. Where is He?

NARRATOR: He's still asleep in the back of the boat.

PUPPET *(rocking back and forth):* Asleep! We're all about to drown, and He's still asleep?

NARRATOR: What are you going to do?

PUPPET: I'm going to wake Him up. Jesus! Wake up! Start bailing! We're about to sink!

NARRATOR: Well, you did it. You woke Him up.

PUPPET *(rocking back and forth):* Good. What's He doing now?

NARRATOR: He's standing up in the front of the boat and saying something.

PUPPET *(rocking back and forth):* What's He saying?

NARRATOR: He says, "Peace. Be still."

PUPPET *(suddenly stops rocking motion. Slowly looks up, down, and all around. Speaks quietly):* Nice night out. *(Almost whispering)* It worked.

NARRATOR: Jesus made the sky, the clouds, the lake, everything. So when He tells them to do something, they do it.

PUPPET: Wow, that's pretty powerful.

NARRATOR: It sure is. But as powerful as Jesus is, He still wants to be your Friend.

PUPPET: Even though I yelled at Him? I would like to be His friend.

NARRATOR: That's good. Jesus will be your Friend, if you ask Him to. Thank you for helping us.

Focus Questions:
1. On what lake did the disciples sail?
2. What had Jesus finished doing just before they boarded the boat?
3. What did Jesus do when He got on board the boat?
4. Why, do you think, didn't Jesus wake up when the storm came?
5. How would you have felt if you were a disciple at the end of this story?

Woman at the Well Trick

Biblical Text: John 4:1-42; Matthew 5:6

Scene Preparation: Talk to the children about the following:
"Think back to sometime when you were really thirsty."
"Have you ever been so thirsty that you would have given just about anything for one drink of water?"
"What will happen if we don't get enough water?"
"That's how it is with our souls. We need spiritual water or else we will die."
For this performance you will need to purchase an inexpensive little trick available at most novelty stores. It comes under various names but is basically a jug or jar that continues to pour out water, after appearing to have been emptied.

Cast: NARRATOR and PUPPET

NARRATOR *(to audience):* Let's see if we can play a trick on one of our puppets, OK? But be very, very quiet. Listen to what I say and to what our puppet says. Are you ready?

(NARRATOR *calls* PUPPET *onto stage.*)

(Enter PUPPET.*)*

PUPPET: What do you want?

NARRATOR: I was wondering if you believe in miracles?

PUPPET: Sure I do.

NARRATOR: Have you ever seen a miracle?

PUPPET: I don't think so.

NARRATOR: I think you might have seen one but just didn't know it. Let me tell you a story about a very big but very quiet miracle.

PUPPET: That sounds interesting.

NARRATOR: OK. Jesus was once traveling through the country of Samaria. He was traveling with His 12 good friends.

PUPPET: You mean His disciples.

13

NARRATOR: Very good! That's right. On the way through Samaria, they stopped at Jacob's Well. Jesus sent His disciples into the town to get some food.

PUPPET: Hit the local Burger Barn, huh?

NARRATOR: Wherever they could find some food.

PUPPET: Sounds good to me. Let's eat!

NARRATOR: Later. Could you tell me what you get out of a well?

(NARRATOR *slowly pours water from jug into a cup until the jug is "empty."*)

PUPPET: Sure! Water!

NARRATOR: Good. While Jesus was waiting for His disciples to come back from town, there came a Samaritan woman to the well to get some . . .

(NARRATOR *slowly pours water from jug into a cup.*)

PUPPET *(puzzled):* Water?! Wait a minute! That was empty! What's going on here?

NARRATOR: That's just the question she asked when Jesus spoke to her. She didn't expect Jesus to even talk to her because He was a Jew, and the Jews hated the Samaritans. So she was very surprised when Jesus asked her for some . . .

(NARRATOR *slowly pours water from jug into a cup.*)

PUPPET *(very puzzled):* Water? I'm getting very confused.

NARRATOR: More than that, this woman was not even liked by the other Samaritans. That's why she came to the well alone. But even though she had done several bad things, when Jesus asked, she still gave Him some . . .

(NARRATOR *slowly pours water from jug into a cup.*)

PUPPET *(staring at cup and then NARRATOR):* . . . Water? That's amazing!

NARRATOR: It sure was! Especially when Jesus started to tell her all about the things she had done. This woman got very scared, because she knew that Jesus shouldn't know about those things. She knew that He was very special. Then Jesus told her that He could give her everlasting . . .

(NARRATOR *slowly pours water.*)

PUPPET *(urgently):* . . . Water!? How do you do that?

NARRATOR: That's just the question the woman asked Jesus. He told her that whatever she pulled out of the well would only quench her thirst for a little while. But for that ache in her heart, that thirst she had deep in her soul, she could have . . .

(NARRATOR *pours.*)

PUPPET *(looking at audience):* Water.

NARRATOR: I wonder if she was able to picture a spring in her heart, flowing forever.

PUPPET *(looking from jug to cup):* I think I get the picture.

NARRATOR: All the woman had to do was ask for this gift, and she did. Then, all the people around her noticed a great change. She told all of them about Jesus and what He gave her—an unending spring of spiritual . . .

(NARRATOR *pours.)*

PUPPET: Water.

NARRATOR *(setting jug down next to* PUPPET): You see, this miracle still happens today. All of us can have that spring of water. All we have to do is ask. Isn't that amazing?

PUPPET *(staring at jug):* It certainly is.

NARRATOR: Well, we'll see you later.

(NARRATOR *exits.)*

PUPPET: Bye!

(PUPPET *stares after* NARRATOR, *then looks back to jug. Repeats the head motion a couple of times. Then the* PUPPET *picks up the jug, examines it, finally tipping it up to look into it and pouring water on itself in the process. Exit* PUPPET, *shaking itself dry.)*

Focus Questions:

1. Where did the woman live that met Jesus at the well?
2. Why did the woman come to the well alone?
3. What was the special thing Jesus wanted to give the woman?
4. How long will the water that Jesus gives, last?
5. How can you get this water?

Helpful Little Boy

Biblical Text: John 6:1-14; Matthew 19:21

Scene Preparation: Ask the children the following questions and wait for responses:

"Where is your favorite place to eat?"

"How much can you eat when you are *really* hungry?"

"Have you ever not eaten for an entire day?"

"What did it feel like?"

"How would you have felt if someone had offered you a dinner from your favorite place after you hadn't had anything to eat all day?"

Read Matthew 19:21. Bring two small fish and five dinner rolls.

Cast: NARRATOR *and* PUPPET (very unhappy)

NARRATOR: Well, it's time for us to tell our Bible story. Do you think I need some help telling this story? Who do you think will help me? Let's see. *(Waits for a few seconds. Then clears throat.)* I said, Let's see! *(Waits a few more seconds, then leans over stage and shouts . . .)* I said, LET'S SEE!

(PUPPET *enters.*)

PUPPET: Hey, lighten up! I heard you.

NARRATOR: What took you so long? Aren't you ready to help me tell today's Bible story?

PUPPET: That's what took me so long. I don't think I want to help with any more stories.

NARRATOR: You don't? Why not?

PUPPET: Well, I really get into the stories, you know, and in the Bible I might get shot at by a giant, drowned in a flood, or smashed by stampeding caribou.

NARRATOR *(to audience):* Caribou? *(Back to* PUPPET*)* Never mind that. I promise you that this is going to be a great story, because it talks about one of your favorite things. Food!

PUPPET: Really? Oh, boy! Cookies for everyone! Where's the food! What's the food! I haven't eaten for at least 15 minutes. I'm starving!

NARRATOR: Hold on a minute. We have to tell the story first.

PUPPET: Well, what are you waiting for! Get that cute little mouth of yours working so that I can get mine working. *(Smacks lips)*

NARRATOR: Jesus told beautiful stories and said many wise and good things. People liked to hear Him talk. He also performed lots of miracles: making the sick people well, the blind see, and the deaf hear. So people followed Him wherever He went to see these things.

PUPPET: Nice story. The end. Bring on the food!

NARRATOR: Now cut that out! Just be a little patient. One day Jesus was way out in the desert. But that didn't stop the people. Thousands of them came out to hear Him. There were 5,000 men, plus many women and children.

PUPPET *(to audience):* Did you hear that! Who could believe that! 5,000 people! *(To* NARRATOR*)* How many is 5,000?

NARRATOR: Well, if you count the number of stars on 100 of our flags, that would be 5,000. Remember, that's only how many men there were, not counting women and children.

PUPPET: Wow! I'd like to have that many hamburgers. . . . Now!

NARRATOR: Speaking of food, this is where the subject of food comes up.

PUPPET: Oh, boy! Wait a minute . . . there's no food out in the desert.

NARRATOR: How right you are. There isn't any food, and it seems that nobody remembered to pack a sack lunch.

PUPPET: No food! Oh, no! I'm starving! Someone find a McDonald's—fast!

NARRATOR: I'm afraid there weren't any restaurants out there. There were all these people, very tired and hungry. Here it was dinnertime, and everybody had missed lunch.

PUPPET: This is terrible. My stomach can't take much more of this. I have to eat at least three times an hour. Somebody think of something fast.

NARRATOR: Nobody could think of an answer. It looked like everyone would go hungry.

PUPPET: I'm so hungry I could eat a cactus.

NARRATOR: But then, there was one little boy. A little boy not much older than some of our boys. Let's say you're that little boy, OK?

PUPPET: All right. I'm a starving little kid. Mommy, I'm hungry! *(Sucks thumb)*

NARRATOR: Quiet, Junior, you have a lunch.

PUPPET: What? How did that happen? I thought nobody had food.

NARRATOR: Well, you were so small and unimportant, nobody thought to ask you. But there you are, with your little Sesame Street lunch box.

PUPPET: All right! Cookies, pizza, hot dogs, hamburgers . . .

NARRATOR *(cuts in):* . . . Two fish and five dinner rolls.

(Long pause as PUPPET *slowly turns to stare at* NARRATOR)

PUPPET: You have got to be kidding. What kind of mommy would pack a lunch like that?

NARRATOR: This boy happened to love fish and dinner rolls.

PUPPET *(sarcastically):* Oh, yummy.

NARRATOR: And so did everyone else out there on that desert.

PUPPET *(clutching an imaginary lunch box):* Get away from me! This is my lunch box! You can't have it! Go chew on a cactus!

NARRATOR: That's not very nice.

PUPPET: Well, I'm sorry, but there's not enough to go around.

NARRATOR *(points offstage):* Look. There's Jesus. He doesn't have anything to eat.

PUPPET: Well . . . *(clutching "lunch box" closer)* . . . I'm sorry about that.

NARRATOR: I see. You know He looks very tired. He's been preaching and working some fantastic miracles all day.

PUPPET: Yeah, He ought to take a break and rest.

NARRATOR: You're right. Too bad. He could use a little bite to eat, but that's just the way it is.

PUPPET: Yeah, too bad.

NARRATOR: You know *(coming closer to* PUPPET *and stage whispering),* there is one person who could give Jesus something to eat.

PUPPET *(astonished):* There is?

NARRATOR: That's right. But that greedy person won't share his lunch with anybody.

PUPPET: No?!?

NARRATOR: That's right. He won't even give some food to the Son of God after all the nice things that He's done for people.

PUPPET *(outraged):* What a rotten person.

NARRATOR: That's right. He ought to march right up there and give his food to Jesus, right?

PUPPET: Right! He ought to march right up there and . . . *(the light dawns)* . . . oops.

NARRATOR: Jesus would just love two fish and five dinner rolls.

PUPPET *(to audience):* What have I done?

NARRATOR: You have just volunteered.

PUPPET *(not too thrilled):* Oh, goody for me. How did I get into this?

(PUPPET *exits.)*

NARRATOR: So the helpful little boy gave his lunch to Jesus, because he loved Jesus and wanted Him to have something to eat.

(PUPPET *enters.)*

PUPPET: That's right. But it would have been nice for someone else to have done it.

NARRATOR: Well, nobody else had any food. Look, Jesus is praying over the food.

PUPPET: That's nice. Everybody should do that before he eats.

NARRATOR: Now, He's breaking the fish and rolls and passing them out among the people.

PUPPET: They won't go very far.

NARRATOR: Oh? Can somebody tell us what happened with that food? *(Wait for a response)* That's right. Everybody had enough to eat.

PUPPET: You mean there was enough for everyone?

NARRATOR: That's right. Jesus multiplied the food so that it would feed all those thousands of people. And you know something else? That little boy took home 12 shopping carts of leftovers full of bread and fish.

PUPPET: Amazing! Fish and bread for everyone. That's enough even for me!

NARRATOR: You know, Jesus made that simple little lunch a lot bigger and better than the little boy thought it could ever be. He can do the same thing with your life.

PUPPET: That's exciting.

NARRATOR: I told you that you would like this story. Thanks for your help.

Focus Questions:

1. How many fish and loaves were there?

2. How many men were there?
3. How many people do you think there were?
4. What did Jesus do just before He passed out the food?
5. Why, do you think, were there so many leftovers?
6. How would you have felt if you were that little boy?
7. How could Jesus make your life bigger and better?

The Things You See on a Lake

Biblical Text: Matthew 14:22-33; Psalm 121:1-2

Scene Preparation: Have wiffle ball (light plastic baseball with holes in it) or a Nerf ball and plastic baseball bat. Call up a child and have him try hitting the ball. Ask everyone, "What is the first rule for hitting the ball?" They should say, "Keep your eye on the ball." Have him hit it first by watching the ball. Then have him try hitting it while looking at the audience, or the window, or something else.

Cast: NARRATOR, PUPPET 1, PUPPET 2, and PUPPET 3

NARRATOR: Here we are again, using our puppets to meet another person who knew Jesus.

(Enter PUPPET 1, *possibly with snorkel and face mask, or maybe* PUPPET 1 *is a fish.)*

PUPPET 1 *(nasal sounding):* I believe that's my cue.

NARRATOR: Well, hello. What's you're name?

PUPPET 1: The name's Sam.

NARRATOR: It's a pleasure to meet you. You look like an interesting character, Sam. What do you do for a living?

PUPPET 1: I'm a fish counter.

NARRATOR: A fish counter?

PUPPET 1: Yeah. I sit at the bottom of a lake and count the fish.

NARRATOR: That sounds very . . . uh . . . boring.

PUPPET 1: No way. You wouldn't believe some of the things I see in my line of work.

NARRATOR: Really?

PUPPET 1: Why I can think back just a little while ago and remember something that would just curl your tail.

21

NARRATOR: That would be a neat trick.

PUPPET 1: There were these men, you see, who were out on my lake. It's so big it's actually called a sea . . . the Sea of Galilee.

NARRATOR: Yes, I think we've heard of it.

PUPPET 1: Anyway, these men were out fishing, and doing a poor job of it may I add.

NARRATOR: I guess you're the expert.

PUPPET 1: Well, this big storm suddenly breaks right over the middle of the lake. These fellows try and try, but they can't get back to shore.

(Exit PUPPET 1. *Enter* PUPPET 2 *and* PUPPET 3. *Any storm sound effects would be appropriate.)*

PUPPET 2: You've really done it this time, Andrew.

PUPPET 3: What did I do? I sure didn't ask this storm to come. Besides, I didn't even want to come fishing tonight, but you made me, big brother.

PUPPET 2: Yeah? It's still your fault. If you weren't so wishy-washy you would have said no, and then I would have stayed home too.

PUPPET 3: Sure, Peter. You would have gotten some other pigeon to come sailing with you. Grab the jib, before it snaps off and washes overboard!

PUPPET 2: Boy, I sure wish Jesus was here.

PUPPET 3: Yeah. We could really use Him now.

NARRATOR *(snapping fingers):* Freeze! (PUPPET 2 *and* PUPPET 3 *stop moving.)* Hey, Sam! *(Enter* PUPPET 1, *staring at* PUPPET 2 *and* PUPPET 3.)

PUPPET 1: Hey, nice trick.

NARRATOR: Never mind that. Can you tell us why these two brothers would like to have Jesus with them. Is He that good of a sailor?

PUPPET 1: Believe it or not, Jesus is a carpenter by trade.

NARRATOR: And why would they want a carpenter with them?

PUPPET 1: Why don't you let them show you?

(PUPPET 1 *exits.)*

NARRATOR: OK. *(Snaps fingers)*

PUPPET 3 *(shouting):* Keep bailing, Peter, or else we'll sink!

PUPPET 2 *(shouting back):* I'm bailing, I'm bailing! Stop using your mouth and start using your hands, Andrew!

PUPPET 3: Peter! Wait a minute! *(Pointing)* Look over there! What is it?

PUPPET 2: I don't know. It looks like a man walking on the water. It must be a spirit or a ghost!

PUPPET 3: No, listen. I can hear Him calling. It's Jesus! He's walking toward us . . . on the water!

NARRATOR *(snaps fingers):* Freeze! (PUPPET 2 *and* PUPPET 3 *stop moving.*) Hey, Sam! Was that really Jesus coming toward them on the water?

(PUPPET 1 *enters.*)

PUPPET 1: It sure was. This man Jesus was more than a carpenter. He is the Son of God. He's done a lot of things more fantastic than walking on the water, but that gets into a lot of other stories. Why don't you let these two finish this one?

(PUPPET 1 *exits.*)

NARRATOR: OK. *(Snapping fingers)*

PUPPET 2: What a guy! Walking on the water! Everything is going to be OK, Andrew. Hmmmm. I wonder if He'd let me walk on the water too.

PUPPET 3: Better not try it, big brother. You always get yourself into trouble with your big ideas.

PUPPET 2: Listen, Andrew, He heard me. He's calling me and motioning me to come to Him. I know I can do it. It seems so simple when I watch Him do it. Here I go! *(Moves away from* PUPPET 3*)*

PUPPET 3: That's it, Peter. Keep your eyes on Jesus! You're doing it!

PUPPET 2: I'm walking on the water! This is great! *(Turning and looking at* PUPPET 3*)* Look, Andrew! *(Starts looking around)*

PUPPET 3: No, Peter! Keep watching Jesus!

PUPPET 2 *(said with wonder):* What a wind! Listen to it! *(Said with uncertainty)* What big waves! Look at them! *(Said with fear)* WHAT AM I DOING! I'M SINKING! (PUPPET 2 *starts "sinking" behind stage.*)

PUPPET 3: Hang in there, Peter! Here comes Jesus. He's going to help you. *(Nagging)* I told you, you should have kept watching Him. I told you, you shouldn't have gone out there. I told you . . .

PUPPET 2: Andrew, be qui . . . blub, blub, blub . . . HELP!

(Exit PUPPET 2 *and* PUPPET 3. *Enter* PUPPET 1.*)*

NARRATOR: Hey, Sam, did Jesus get there in time?

PUPPET 1: Of course. But you see Peter's whole problem started when he stopped watching Jesus. He started looking at the waves and at the people watching him.

NARRATOR: But he did have the faith to start walking on the water.

PUPPET 1: Sure. That's the way it is with life. We have to keep our eyes on Jesus if we are to keep the faith that we had when we first started following Him.

NARRATOR: And when we have problems we should continue watching Jesus, and He can give us strength to come through our problems.

PUPPET 1: Right. And one way to keep from having as many problems is to follow *before* we get into trouble.

NARRATOR: You were right, Sam. That was exciting.

PUPPET 1: I'm glad you enjoyed it. You'll find a lot more like that in the Bible. Well, I'll be seeing you.

(PUPPET 1 *exits.)*

NARRATOR: Thanks, Sam. Happy fish counting.

Focus Questions:

1. What did the disciples think Jesus was when they first saw Him walking on the water?
2. Which disciple walked on the water?
3. Why did Peter begin to sink?
4. Why, do you think, was Peter able to walk on the water?
5. How, do you think, did it feel to walk on the water?

Zacchaeus

Biblical Text: Luke 19:1-10; Matthew 18:11

Scene Preparation: Ask the children the following questions:
"Is there anybody you don't like?"
"What does he do that you don't like?"
"Do you know somebody who doesn't like you?"
"Why, do you think, doesn't he like you?"
NARRATOR will need cue cards that say, "Boo," "Yeah," and "Murmur." The puppet stage needs a raised area decorated and/or labeled "tree.")

Cast: NARRATOR and PUPPET

NARRATOR *(to audience):* This is going to be a special story today because we need you to be a part of it. You are going to be the crowd. Let's try saying our lines together. First, we need to say "Boo!" Altogether now *(with cue card),* BOO! Now, let's try saying "Yeah!" *(with cue card).* Now let's try murmuring together, "murmur, murmur, murmur" *(with cue card).* Good. Let's start our story.

(Enter PUPPET.)

PUPPET *(in a very "nasty" mood):* Let's not, and say we did. I just want to go home.

NARRATOR: That wouldn't be right. These kids deserve a story.

PUPPET: What did they ever do for me?

NARRATOR: That sounds pretty selfish.

PUPPET: Why should I care?

NARRATOR: Don't you care about other people?

PUPPET: Nah. I'm too busy looking after number one . . . me!

NARRATOR: That attitude sounds pretty small to me.

PUPPET: Hey! Watch the short jokes, OK?

NARRATOR: Short jokes? Oh, you are sort of small, aren't you?

PUPPET: Lay off!

NARRATOR: Who are you, anyway?

PUPPET: The name's Zacchaeus.

NARRATOR: Zacchaeus, the tax collector?

PUPPET: That's right. I'm the best tax collector in Jericho. Nobody can collect more taxes than me.

NARRATOR: That must make you feel like a pretty *big* man.

PUPPET: Look, just cool the comments on my size.

NARRATOR: Sounds like you still aren't very happy.

PUPPET: What do you mean? I'm successful, I'm rich, I'm popular. . . .

NARRATOR: Popular?

PUPPET: Sure! I throw some of the biggest parties this side of the Jordan River. I have hundreds of people come.

NARRATOR: Really? How many of those people even talk to you after the party?

PUPPET: Well . . . uh . . . some . . .

NARRATOR: How many?

PUPPET: . . . Uh . . . a few . . .

NARRATOR: How many?

PUPPET: None.

NARRATOR: I wonder why?

PUPPET: I thought, maybe, I forgot to leave the onions off my cheeseburger.

NARRATOR *(to audience):* It seems that wherever Zacchaeus went the crowds would say . . . *(Hold up "Boo" cue card.)* It sounds kind of lonely.

PUPPET: It doesn't bother me . . . much.

NARRATOR: You're not very happy, are you, Zacchaeus?

PUPPET: Well, I could be a little happier.

NARRATOR: I wonder what we could do about it?

PUPPET: Well, I do have an idea. There's this man, Jesus, who seems to bring joy to everyone who comes to Him. He's coming here to Jericho today. Maybe I could talk to Him.

(Exit PUPPET.)

NARRATOR: That sounds like a good idea. So, Zacchaeus ran out to the city gate where Jesus would be entering. When he got there, he couldn't even get close to the gate, because there was such a crowd.

(Enter PUPPET.*)*

PUPPET: Good grief! I can't even see past the back row. What am I going to do?

NARRATOR: Well, you could climb that sycamore tree.

PUPPET *(looking at tree and back to* NARRATOR*):* Forget it. I don't like heights.

NARRATOR: That's the only way you're going to see Jesus.

PUPPET: I'm not climbing any dumb tree.

NARRATOR *(getting forceful):* Look, I've been very patient so far. In the story you climb that sycamore tree to see Jesus. Now, let's get climbing!

PUPPET: Let's not, and say we did.

NARRATOR: Climb!

PUPPET: All right! All right! You don't have to get an attitude. (PUPPET *moves up to higher platform.)* Here I am. Feeling like a dumb bird.

NARRATOR: Then Zacchaeus heard the crowd cheer as Jesus came into town. *(Hold up cue card that says "Yeah!")* Zacchaeus didn't say a thing as Jesus approached.

PUPPET: Of course not. He was too scared being up in this dumb tree.

NARRATOR: Then Jesus stopped and looked up into the tree. At first the crowd didn't know why. . . .

PUPPET: It's a mystery to me. Why would anyone stop to see a scared tax collector clinging for his life in a sycamore tree?

NARRATOR: . . . But then Jesus said, "Zacchaeus, come down. I am going to your house for lunch today."

PUPPET: Really? Who's buying?

NARRATOR: Zacchaeus was thrilled and quickly came down from the tree.

PUPPET: All right! *(Looking around)* Uh . . . let's see . . . how do I get down. Maybe this way . . . YAAAHH! (PUPPET *drops out of sight with a crash.)*

NARRATOR: Well, that's one way to get down. When they heard that Jesus was going to have dinner with Zacchaeus, the tax collector, the crowd started murmuring among themselves. *(Cue audience)* They thought it very strange that such a good man, like Jesus, would take time to be with such a sinner, like Zacchaeus. But after dinner, they found that Zacchaeus had changed.

PUPPET *(with gentle voice):* Listen, everyone. I'm sorry for all the bad things that I've done. Jesus has shown me how I should live. He has changed me. Anyone that I have cheated, I'll pay back four times what I took from you.

NARRATOR: The crowd cheered . . . *(cue audience with "Yeah" card)* . . . and the new Zacchaeus found that not only did he have Jesus as a friend but also many other new friends because of his new life that started with Jesus' visit.

Focus Questions:

1. What did Zacchaeus do for a living?
2. Why was he unhappy?
3. Why couldn't Zacchaeus see Jesus?
4. What, do you think, did the people say when Jesus went to lunch with Zacchaeus?
5. What, do you think, did the people say when Zacchaeus made his announcement?
6. One of Jesus' disciples was a tax collector. Do you know which one?

The Unhappy Undertaker

Biblical Text: John 11:1-45; 1 Corinthians 15:55

Scene Preparation: Read 1 Corinthians 15:55. Ask the children the following questions and take some responses:
"Has anybody here ever lost a pet or a favorite toy?"
"Have you ever found a pet or toy you thought was lost forever?"
"What were your feelings like?"

Cast: NARRATOR, HORACE, and CALEB

NARRATOR: I wonder what our story is going to be about today. I know just about as much as you do . . . maybe less.

HORACE: Good morning.

NARRATOR: Well, good morning to you too. Who are you?

HORACE *(drearily):* My name is Horace. I'm the benefactor of the bereaved of Bethany.

NARRATOR: What?

HORACE: I'm the undertaker around here.

NARRATOR: Oh, I take it that we are in Bethany?

HORACE: That's correct. Just five miles east of Jerusalem.

NARRATOR: That's very interesting. You sound kind of sad.

HORACE: Well, not really. It's just part of my business, and business has been very good. In fact I have made several interments just recently.

NARRATOR: Say what?

HORACE: I've buried a lot of bods, babe.

NARRATOR: Nobody I know, I hope.

HORACE: Oh, I doubt it. My last one was a gentleman named Lazarus. He is survived by his two sisters, Mary and Martha.

NARRATOR: Wasn't he a very good friend of Jesus of Nazareth?

HORACE: That traveling troublemaker? I guess he was. In fact Jesus was invited to the funeral, but I hear He just got into town today to pay His last respects.

NARRATOR: That ought to be interesting.

HORACE: I doubt it. That funeral was over four days ago. Not much you can do to liven up a funeral. That's a little undertaker humor.

NARRATOR: With a sense of humor like that, I can't see how you get much business.

HORACE: Very simple. I give a double-your-money-back guarantee. Once we bury someone, if they don't stay buried, you get double your money back.

NARRATOR: I still don't see how you can get much business.

HORACE: Well, I am the only undertaker in town.

NARRATOR: Now I understand.

HORACE: Here's my card. If you die, just call me and I'll take care of everything.

NARRATOR: Over my dead body.

HORACE: It does work best that way.

(Exit HORACE.*)*

NARRATOR: Thanks a lot. I wonder who else we can meet.

(Enter CALEB *with microphone.)*

CALEB: Good morning, ladies and gentlemen. This is Caleb Crankcase of BBS.

NARRATOR: Caleb Crankcase? What are you doing here?

CALEB: This is my job. I cover as many newsworthy events as possible for the Bethany Broadcasting Service.

NARRATOR: What's so newsworthy around here?

CALEB: That man Jesus is news, and He's coming here today. Hey, are you busy?

NARRATOR: Not very, why?

CALEB: I need someone to help me report the facts. Sort of a faithful sidekick.

NARRATOR: Like the Lone Ranger and Tonto?

CALEB: More like Roy Rogers and Trigger. It's no problem. The action's going to happen right over there in that cemetery.

NARRATOR: I don't know about this.

CALEB: Stand by, we're coming out of the commercial. Caleb Crankcase here for BBS news. We're here at the city cemetery continuing the coverage of the character called Jesus Christ. Some people call Him a prophet, and others a madman, and some even the Son of God. Let me ask my broadcasting partner, what do you think? *(Holds microphone to* NARRATOR*)*

NARRATOR: Well, Caleb . . .

CALEB *(pulling microphone back):* Thank you. I think we can see a crowd coming now. Yes, I can see Jesus at the front of the crowd. What do you think He might do, here? *(Holds microphone to* NARRATOR*)*

NARRATOR: Well, I think . . .

CALEB *(pulling microphone back):* Thank you. Now we can see Jesus approaching Mary and Martha, the two sisters of the dead man *(can't remember name)* . . . uh . . . uh . . .

NARRATOR *(pulling microphone):* Lazarus.

CALEB *(pulling microphone back):* Watch it. Nobody asked you to . . . wait . . . I can't believe it. But I can see very clearly that Jesus is crying.

NARRATOR: Big deal.

CALEB: Doesn't it seem strange that a person of Jesus' obvious power should cry?

NARRATOR: No. He's sad, so He cries. So what?

CALEB: Uh . . . well . . . I . . . ladies and gentlemen there are further developments. Jesus seems to have asked them to remove the stone from the front of the tomb of His friend . . . uh . . . uh . . .

NARRATOR *(pulling microphone):* Lazarus.

CALEB *(pulling microphone back):* Would you stop doing that! It seems that Jesus wants one last look at His friend. . . . Wait. . . . He seems to be praying out loud, calling God His Father.

NARRATOR: I think He's going to perform a miracle.

CALEB *(staring):* Look, let's keep this broadcast believable, OK? Wait, Jesus is speaking. He just said, "Lazarus! Come out!" The poor man must be overcome by grief and . . . *(stares open-mouthed while the* NARRATOR *smiles at him)* . . . I don't believe it! Lazarus has come out of the tomb, and they are unwrapping him! He's alive!

NARRATOR: Isn't that great!

CALEB: It sure is! This is the opportunity of a lifetime. I get to interview a man who can tell us what it's like to be dead! *(Exits)* Lazarus! Lazarus! This is Caleb Crankcase, BBS news. . . .

NARRATOR *(to audience):* This has been just a little different today kids, but I think we're through with our story, so . . .

(Enter HORACE.*)*

HORACE *(crying):* Ruined! I'm ruined! Nobody wants an undertaker who can't keep them buried.

NARRATOR: What about giving Mary and Martha double their money back?

HORACE: I can only say one thing about that.

NARRATOR: Oh, what's that?

HORACE *(screaming cry):* WAAAAHH!

(Exit HORACE.*)*

NARRATOR *(with finality):* Now, I think this story is over.

Focus questions:
1. In what city did this story happen?
2. How long had Lazarus been dead before Jesus came?
3. What did Jesus do when He met Mary and Martha in Bethany after Lazarus had died?
4. Why, do you think, did Jesus do this?
5. What question would you want to ask Lazarus right after Jesus raised him from the dead?

The Wise Man and the Foolish Man

Biblical Text: Matthew 7:24-27; Proverbs 14:16

Scene Preparation: Bring in two pop bottles. Set them both up, one normal and the other upside down. You might say, "Here we have two identical bottles. Which one will fall down the easiest? Does someone think he can blow one down?" (You might refer to the story of the three little pigs. Ask who was the wisest pig.) Read Proverbs 14:16. "God can keep us steady. Without Him we're doing a balancing act, and it doesn't take much for the devil to push us over." Optional sound effects for this skit are hammering, sawing, and storm noises.

Cast: NARRATOR, PUPPET 1, and PUPPET 2

NARRATOR: The things Jesus said are taken two different ways by people. They either ignore them or try to live by them. This is a story Jesus told to show these two different kinds of people. He used a wise man and a foolish man in this story. Those who ignore His words are like a foolish man.

(Enter PUPPET 1.)

PUPPET 1: Yup, yup, yup, yup. Wow! Look at all the people!

NARRATOR: Let's get on with the story.

PUPPET 1: What story?

NARRATOR: The story that you're in today.

PUPPET 1 *(astonished):* Me! I get to be in a story!?! I'm a star! Ma will be so proud of me. Yup, yup, yup, yup.

NARRATOR *(to audience):* Can anybody guess what part he plays in our story today?

PUPPET 1: Uh, let's see now. That's a tough one. Who could I be?

NARRATOR *(responding to audience):* That's right. He's the foolish man.

PUPPET 1: Hold on there a minute. I resen . . . I reset . . . I . . . I don't like that!

NARRATOR: You don't like being called the foolish man?

PUPPET 1: That's right! My parents gave me a good name, and it ain't "Foolish Man." They knowed me better than that.

NARRATOR: Well, then, we'll call you by your name. What is it?

PUPPET 1: What's what?

NARRATOR: Your name!

PUPPET 1: Oh, that! Dum-Dum.

NARRATOR *(nodding):* You're right. Your parents did know you better than we do.

PUPPET 1: Yup, yup, yup, yup. Uh . . . now, what am I supposed to do?

NARRATOR: In our story, you're supposed to build a house.

PUPPET 1: Oh, goody! *(Sing-song)* I get to build a housey. I get to build a housey. I get to build a housey. I get to build a . . .

NARRATOR *(breaking in):* Hurry up!

PUPPET 1: No need to lose your temper.

NARRATOR: Just pick a spot to build, OK?

PUPPET 1 *(moving to stage right):* Hmmm. Where should I build it? *(Feels stage)* Wow! It's as hard as a rock here!

NARRATOR: Probably because that is rock.

PUPPET 1: Yup, yup, yup, yup. That could be the reason. *(Moves to stage left)* Let's try over here. *(Feels stage)* Oh, that's much nicer. Nice and sandy.

NARRATOR: Why do you want it sandy?

PUPPET 1: Why, because I can dig a whole lot easier in the sand. I can get my house built in no time.

NARRATOR: I see.

PUPPET 1: Yup, yup, yup, yup. I ain't no dummy.

(Exit PUPPET 1.)

NARRATOR: Time will tell. *(To audience)* There was also a wise man in our story.

(Enter PUPPET 2.)

PUPPET 2: . . . And the cube root of the tangent of the equilateral triangle, equals . . .

NARRATOR: Excuse me. You must be the wise man.

PUPPET 2: Oh, yes indeed. I am the wise man.

34

NARRATOR: Exactly how wise are you?

PUPPET 2: Let me give you a little demonstration. Take 500 milliliters of ground triticum, plus 6 grams sodium benzoate, add 500 milliliters sodium chloride, 10 milliliters vegetable petro-extract, and ½ liter H_2O.

NARRATOR: Is that the formula for rocket fuel, or maybe a wonder drug?

PUPPET 2: Oh, no. Nothing as trivial as that.

NARRATOR: Perhaps it is the directions for the construction of a computer chip?

PUPPET 2: Of course not. Follow my directions, and you will come up with one of the most important inventions in history!

NARRATOR: What would that be?

PUPPET 2: Play-Doh.

NARRATOR: That's wisdom?

PUPPET 2: Well, true wisdom is not knowledge but how you use your knowledge.

NARRATOR: Not bad.

PUPPET 2: I just made that up.

NARRATOR: Why don't you build your house, Einstein.

PUPPET 2: Certainly. *(Moves to stage left)* Let's see what it's like over here. *(Feels stage)* Oh, no. That will never do. That's much too sandy. *(Moves to stage right)* We had better try over here. *(Feels stage)* Oh, yes. That's much better.

NARRATOR: But isn't that solid rock?

PUPPET 2: As solid as it comes.

NARRATOR: But won't it be harder to build there?

PUPPET 2: Sure. Any dum-dum knows it's easier to build on sand than rock. But when I'm done with my house it will be able to stand up against earthquakes, tornadoes, floods, and even stampeding caribou!

NARRATOR: I see. Well, good luck with your house.

PUPPET 2: Thank you.

(Exit PUPPET 2. *The sounds of hammering and sawing are heard backstage.)*

NARRATOR: So the wise man and foolish man . . .

PUPPET 1 *(from offstage):* That's Dum-Dum.

NARRATOR: Excuse me. The wise man and Dum-Dum started building their homes. They both used the same lumber and bricks. The only difference was that the wise man built his house on the rock, and Dum-Dum built his house on the sand. Dum-Dum finished first.

(Enter PUPPET 1.)

PUPPET 1: Yeah! I win!

NARRATOR: How do you like your house?

PUPPET 1: Well let me show you some pictures. *(Gives NARRATOR pictures as he talks.)* Here's my kitchen. Like the colors?

NARRATOR *(rubbing eyes):* Well, I have to admit, black with bright orange and purple daisies would help me with my diet.

PUPPET 1: Ma will be so proud. Here's my master bedroom. I like how the grass grows right up through the floor.

NARRATOR: It does make an interesting shag carpet.

PUPPET 1: And here is my favorite . . . the sunken living room.

NARRATOR *(handing back pictures):* Unusual. But I must say, it's you.

PUPPET 1: Thank you. Come over anytime, except Monday. That's when I mow my bedroom. Yup, yup, yup, yup.

(Exit PUPPET 1.)

NARRATOR *(to audience):* Some time afterward, the wise man finished his house.

(Enter PUPPET 2.)

PUPPET 2: It was hard work, but it was worth it, now that I'm moved in.

NARRATOR: It looks like you finished just in time. There seems to be a big storm coming.

PUPPET 2: No problem. My house can stand anything.

NARRATOR: I sure hope so. *(Sound effects)* Listen to that wind.

PUPPET 2: Sounds somewhat like a Rachmaninoff piano concerto.

NARRATOR: Here comes the rain!

PUPPET 2: If you'll excuse me, I enjoy observing the interesting geometric patterns raindrops form on my windows.

(Exit PUPPET 2.)

NARRATOR: He certainly seems to have everything under control here. Let's go see how Dum-Dum's doing.

(Enter PUPPET 1.)

PUPPET 1: Howdy! Looks like a storm is on its way. Yup, yup, yup, yup.

NARRATOR: You're right. Here comes the wind.

PUPPET 1 *(starting to sway back and forth):* Rock-a-bye, Dum-Dum, in the treetop . . .

NARRATOR: Here comes the rain. Boy, it's coming down hard.

PUPPET 1: Yup, yup, yup . . . oh, oh . . . I think my sunken living room is sinking.

NARRATOR *(to audience):* When the wind and rain hit Dum-Dum's house, do you know what happened?

PUPPET 1: The big, bad wolf huffed and puffed. . . .

NARRATOR: Not in this story, Dum-Dum. *(To audience)* What happened? *(Take response if one is given.)* Right. The sand gave away. And the house fell down and was swept away by the flood.

PUPPET 1: Yup, yup, yup *(sinking),* blub, blub, blub. . . .

(PUPPET 1 *exits.)*

NARRATOR: But the wise man's house stood firm on the rock. So the wise man stayed warm and dry and safe.

(Enter PUPPET 2.)

PUPPET 2: I love a story with a happy ending.

NARRATOR: Wise man, could you tell us what Jesus wanted us to learn from this story?

PUPPET 2: Why, I should think it is clear. When bad things happen to us and we don't have our lives built on Jesus, our lives will fall flat, just like Dum-Dum's house. But if we have our lives built on Jesus, then they stand up firm and strong.

(Exit PUPPET 2.)

NARRATOR: That's right. So kids, be like the wise man, not the foolish man. . . .

PUPPET 1 *(from offstage):* That's Dum-Dum!

NARRATOR: Whatever.

Focus Questions:
1. Where did the wise man build his house?
2. Where did the foolish man build his house?
3. Why did the foolish man build his house there?
4. Which house was stronger?
5. Who does the rock represent?
6. What are some things in your life that are like the wind and rain?

Forgiveness

Biblical Test: Matthew 18:21-22; Colossians 3:13

Scene Preparation: Say something like this, "Imagine that you are playing a game with someone. It seems that every time you play a game with this person, he cheats or does something bad. How many times would you let this happen before you stop playing with that person?"

Cast: NARRATOR and MONSTER *(preferably with a sweet attitude)*

NARRATOR: Today I would like to speak to you about forgiveness. I thought we would look in the Bible and see what Jesus had to say about forgiveness. We found that Peter, who was one of Jesus' disciples, asked Jesus if we should forgive seven times. But Jesus said, "Not seven times, but seventy times seven." That's a lot of forgiveness. I thought maybe you would like to see how much seventy times seven is, so I set my chalkboard and chalk . . . *(turns to stage)* . . . right . . . here? My chalkboard. My chalk. I'm sure I set it up right here. Where could it be? *(To audience)* Excuse me for just a moment, please. I'll be right back.

(Exit NARRATOR behind puppet stage, or offstage. After a couple of seconds, enter MONSTER eating a piece of chalk.)

MONSTER: This pretty good stuff. A little dry, but pretty good. *(To audience)* You know what me find? Me find big, black, square flat thing. It remind me of big, black cookie. So monster eat it. Then me find furry, black, square thing. And monster eat that too. Now, me on dessert. Me think they were little white peppermint sticks. Too dusty. Not very minty. Me wonder what they were. Do you know what big, black, square cookie was? Do you know what furry, black, square thing was? Do you know what little, dusty, white things were?

(MONSTER should interact with audience so they tell him that he just ate chalkboard, eraser, and chalk.)

NARRATOR *(from offstage):* I don't know what could have happened. I can't find the chalkboard, the eraser, or the chalk. All I can find is this trail of chalk dust.

MONSTER *(alarmed):* Uh-oh. Me think monster just get into bad trouble.

NARRATOR *(from offstage):* Somebody must have taken them. Boy, if I find them, they're really going to be sorry!

MONSTER: Me sorry now! What monster going to do? Me always eating things.

(Enter NARRATOR.*)*

NARRATOR: I don't understand it. I can't find them anywhere. It's almost like something just swallowed them up. (MONSTER *stares at audience and starts to shake all over.)* All I can find is chalk dust. (MONSTER *looks at hands, coughs, and covers mouth.* NARRATOR *finally notices* MONSTER.*)* Oh, hi, Monster. Say, you wouldn't now what happened to my chalkboard, eraser, and chalk, would you?

MONSTER: Mumble, mumble, mumble, mumble.

NARRATOR: I can't quite make out what you're saying, Monster. Can you help me? I need those things for my talk on forgiveness.

MONSTER *(shrugs):* Mumble, mumble, mumble *(shakes head)*. Mumble, mumble, mumble.

NARRATOR: I can't understand you, Monster. Open your mouth and speak up.

MONSTER: Mumble, mumble, mumble, bad breath.

NARRATOR: I see. *(Turns to audience.* MONSTER *frantically rubs his hands and mouth as if to remove the chalk dust.)* Well, as I said, Jesus told us that we should forgive each other not 7 times but 70 times 7. *(Turning to* MONSTER, *who is startled and tries to act normal)* Do you know how much that is, Monster?

MONSTER *(shaking head very quickly):* Mumble, mumble, mumble.

NARRATOR *(turns to audience.* MONSTER *resumes actions):* I really wonder if Jesus wanted us to count the number of times we forgave a person, or if He meant we should always be willing to forgive them. *(Turning to* MONSTER, *who again tries to act normal)* What do you think, Monster?

MONSTER *(shrugs):* Mumble, mumble, mumble.

NARRATOR *(aside to audience):* I don't get it. What's wrong with Monster? (NARRATOR *should interact with audience to find out that* MONSTER *ate his things.)* He did what? Really? Let's see. *(Moving to* MONSTER *who closes his mouth, turns his head away, and hides his hands.)* How are things going, Monster?

MONSTER *(shrugs):* Mumble, mumble, mumble.

NARRATOR *(nodding):* I see. *(Here the* NARRATOR *and* MONSTER *could have some fun. When* NARRATOR *turns away,* MONSTER *could turn back to look at him. But when* NARRATOR *turns back toward* MONSTER, MONSTER *turns away. Play it for laughs. Finally the* NARRATOR *should look up and point.)* Look! Up there! A giant, flying, chocolate chip cookie!

MONSTER *(forgetting his problem, looks up):* Where?

NARRATOR *(turning and looking into* MONSTER'S *mouth):* Aha! Chalkdust!

MONSTER *(covering mouth):* Oh, oh.

NARRATOR *(very angry):* Well, you've done it again, haven't you! You eat my flowers! You eat my furniture, and you eat my records! What am I going to do with you!

MONSTER *(lowering head):* Monster sorry.

NARRATOR: You are always sorry, Monster! It's not enough you eat my things at home, but now you eat the things I needed to talk about forgiveness!

MONSTER: Excuse me?

NARRATOR: WHAT!

MONSTER: What is forgiveness?

NARRATOR *(pauses for a long time and looks at the audience):* Well . . . you see . . . I guess you'd say it's when someone does something bad. . . .

MONSTER: Like eating big, black, flat, square cookie?

NARRATOR *(nodding):* Yeah, I guess so. Anyway, you decide to forget that it ever happened.

MONSTER: Forgiveness sound nice to Monster.

NARRATOR *(dryly):* I bet it does.

MONSTER: How we get forgiveness to work?

NARRATOR: Well, one person needs to ask to be forgiven.

MONSTER: Like me wish Monster would be forgiven?

NARRATOR: Yes. Then you need someone who is willing to do the forgiving. But, Monster, you are always eating or breaking my things. I don't know how many times I've already forgiven you.

MONSTER: Seventy times seven? (MONSTER *stares at* NARRATOR, *who looks at audience, then back at* MONSTER *two or three times.)*

NARRATOR: All right, all right. I forgive you.

MONSTER: Oh, thank you, thank you. (MONSTER *kisses* NARRATOR.) You not be sorry. Monster be good.

NARRATOR: Fine, fine. Why doesn't Monster go be good some place else right now.

MONSTER: Oh, sure. Me go. Bye, bye.

(Exit MONSTER.)

NARRATOR *(to audience):* I guess this was better than any old chalk talk. You were able to see forgiveness really happen. Sometime this week you will probably need to forgive someone. When you do, it will probably make you feel good, so . . . *(Loud crunch heard from offstage.* NARRATOR *looks back and rubs head with hand.)* . . . my new tape player. We better stop now kids, before I reach 71 times 7. *(As* NARRATOR *exits)* Monster! Get away from there!

Focus Questions:

1. How many times did Peter think we should forgive someone?
2. How many times did Jesus say we should forgive someone?
3. Should we really keep track of how many times we forgive someone?
4. What does forgiveness really mean?
5. Besides forgiving someone, what else can we do to make them a better person?

Who Owes Whom?

Biblical Text: Matthew 18:23-35; Luke 17:3-4

Scene Preparation: Ask the children the following questions:
"How many of you have let someone borrow something from you?"
"Did you get it back every time?"
"If you didn't get it back, what did you do?"
"Did you ever borrow something from someone, then couldn't give it back?
What happened?"

Cast: NARRATOR, PUPPET 1, PUPPET 2, and PUPPET 3

NARRATOR: The Lord's Prayer says "forgive us our debts, as we forgive our debtors." We want to tell you a little story about forgiveness. Jesus started this story with a man who was very wealthy . . .

(Enter PUPPET 1 *and* PUPPET 2.*)*

PUPPET 1: . . . And very generous.

PUPPET 2: I'm sure glad to hear that.

NARRATOR: Why is that?

PUPPET 2: I need to borrow some money.

PUPPET 1: Don't I know you?

PUPPET 2: I work for one of your companies. In fact, I'm one of your vice presidents in charge of widget production.

PUPPET 1: Oh, yes. Now I remember. What can I do for you?

PUPPET 2: You see, I have a very important business deal, and I need to borrow some money from you, just a little.

PUPPET 1: How little is little?

PUPPET 2: Uh . . . about $5 million.

PUPPET 1 *(gulp):* Wow! Little isn't what it used to be.

42

PUPPET 2: I know it really is a lot of money, but I can pay you back in just one month, honest. If I don't pay you back, you can throw me into prison.

PUPPET 1: I'd rather have my money.

PUPPET 2: You'll get it, I promise.

PUPPET 1: OK. You look trustworthy. Let's go see my banker.

(Exit PUPPETS.)

NARRATOR: So the very wealthy and generous man loaned his vice president $5 million. The loan would be paid back in one month; the vice president guaranteed it. But at the end of one month . . .

(Enter PUPPET 2.)

PUPPET 2: Shhhh!

NARRATOR: What's wrong?

PUPPET 2 *(whispering):* Have you seen my boss?

NARRATOR: No, but I could find him for you.

PUPPET 2 *(whispering):* No, no, no. Don't bother.

NARRATOR: Oh, it's no bother. *(Starts to look around)*

PUPPET 2 *(whispering urgently):* Don't do that!

NARRATOR: What's wrong? Don't you want to see him?

PUPPET 2 *(whispering):* No.

NARRATOR: I thought you were supposed to meet him today to pay back the $5 million you owe him.

PUPPET 2 *(whispering):* I know, I know. That's the problem. I don't have the money.

NARRATOR: You don't have it! What happened?

PUPPET 2 *(whispering):* My business deal fell flat. I'm broke.

NARRATOR: Oh, no! That means he can have you thrown into prison. He can take everything you own.

PUPPET 2: I know, I know. (PUPPET 1 *enters from behind* PUPPET 2.) So don't tell him you saw me. *(Starts backing away from* NARRATOR, *toward* PUPPET 1) I'll just be leaving, now. I think I'll go to Mexico or . . . *(Bumping into* PUPPET 1) . . . Aaaah!

PUPPET 1: Hi, there, Mr. Vice President! Sorry I missed you earlier. I know you've been looking for me. I'm sometimes hard to find.

PUPPET 2: Not hard enough, it seems.

PUPPET 1: Well . . .

PUPPET 2: Uh . . . well, what?

PUPPET 1: My money.

PUPPET 2: Uh . . . what money is that?

PUPPET 1 *(stares at audience for a moment):* As much as I'd love to continue this marvelous conversation, I would like to have my $5 million back, please.

PUPPET 2: Oh, that money!

PUPPET 1: Yes, where is it?

PUPPET 2: Well, it . . . mumble mumble mumble.

PUPPET 1: Excuse me?

PUPPET 2: It . . . mumble mumble mumble.

PUPPET 1: I still can't understand you.

NARRATOR: He said he doesn't have the money.

PUPPET 1: Oh. Is that all. I just couldn't understand what he was . . . Doesn't have the money!

PUPPET 2 *(to* NARRATOR*):* Thanks a lot.

NARRATOR: My pleasure.

PUPPET 1: That was $5 million. That's a lot of widgets! I guess you know what this means.

PUPPET 2: No, please! I don't want to go to prison. Please, I'll try to pay you back. Maybe five dollars a month for a million months? *(Crying)* I'll be your slave, please. . . .

PUPPET 1: I don't want a slave, I want my money.

PUPPET 2: I'll do anything. I'll kiss your feet.

PUPPET 1: Over my dead body!

PUPPET 2: PLEASE DON'T SEND ME TO PRISON!

PUPPET 1: OK.

PUPPET 2: PLEASE DON'T . . . what?

PUPPET 1: Why don't we just forget about the whole thing?

PUPPET 2: You mean it?

PUPPET 1: Sure. (PUPPET 1 *starts to exit.)*

PUPPET 2: Oh, thank you, thank you, thank you.

(PUPPET 2 *follows* PUPPET 1, *kissing him.*)

PUPPET 1: Would you stop doing that!

(Exit PUPPETS.*)*

NARRATOR: Well, it just so happened that two months before, a worker had borrowed five dollars from this same vice president. Today was the collection day.

(Enter PUPPET 2 *from stage right and* PUPPET 3 *from stage left.)*

PUPPET 2 *(angry):* There you are. Where's my five bucks?

PUPPET 3 *(scared):* I'm . . . I'm . . . I'm sorry, sir. I don't have it right now. I should have it tomorrow.

PUPPET 2: That's not soon enough. *(Enter* PUPPET 1 *from stage right, behind* PUPPET 2.) I want that five dollars right now.

PUPPET 3: But sir, I don't have it. Give me just a little more time!

PUPPET 2: Forget it! You're fired! I don't hire deadbeats.

PUPPET 3: Please, sir. Give me another chance. I can get it.

PUPPET 2: No way! Only a fool would let someone get away with a bad debt. *(Knocks* PUPPET 3 *off the stage.)* I'm sending the police after you! Then, I'm taking that five bucks out of your hide. *(Turning around)* Then, I'm . . . *(Seeing* PUPPET 1) . . . I'm . . . I'm in deep trouble.

PUPPET 1: Since you're going to be talking to the police, could you tell them I want a certain person who owes me $5 million picked up? I believe he's one of my vice presidents.

PUPPET 2: But, boss, you said that you were going to forget that debt.

PUPPET 1: If you can't forget a little debt like five dollars, how can I forget a debt like $5 million. After all, only a fool would let someone get away with a bad debt. Let's go see the police.

PUPPET 2: Please, boss. I'll . . .

PUPPET 1: And if you start kissing me again, the police will be the least of your worries!

(Exit PUPPETS.*)*

NARRATOR: Since God forgives us, He wants us to forgive others. Let's remember that God is happy when we forgive, but He is sad with us when we don't.

Focus Questions:

1. Who owed whom the most money?
2. What did the wealthy man do about the debt?

3. How much did the third man owe the vice president?
4. What made the wealthy man change his mind about forgiving the debt?
5. If you could change this story, what would you change?

The Good Samarimonster

Biblical Text: Luke 10:30-37; Romans 13:8

Scene Preparation: On a board or large piece of paper, list the qualities of a good neighbor, or friend, as the children give them to you. You will need a hockey puck or some black round thing.

Cast: NARRATOR, PUPPET 1, PUPPET 2, PUPPET 3, PUPPET 4, and MONSTER

NARRATOR: Once upon a time there lived a . . .

(Enter PUPPET 1.)

PUPPET 1: Salesman! Herman T. Frogsworth at your service.

NARRATOR: A very successful salesman.

PUPPET 1: Top salesman for Pendale Hockey Pucks.

NARRATOR: Pendale Hockey Pucks?

PUPPET 1: That's what I said. *(Looking eye to eye with* NARRATOR) "Pick a Pendale, and you've picked the perfect puck."

NARRATOR *(wiping face):* Right. He was about to head down to Jericho after a big sale in Jerusalem.

PUPPET 1: That's right. Two thousand hockey pucks to the Jerusalem Jets; 200 shekels in commission.

NARRATOR: Off he started, down the road to Jericho alone, in spite of the warnings of his friends.

PUPPET 1: They worry too much.

NARRATOR: They had told him how dangerous it was to go down that road alone.

PUPPET 1: Ridiculous!

NARRATOR: They said he would probably be mugged and robbed.

47

PUPPET 1: Nonsense! There probably isn't a mugger or a robber within 100 miles of me. *(Enter* PUPPET 2.) There's nothing to worry about.

NARRATOR: Are you sure?

PUPPET 1: Sure I'm . . . *(Sees* PUPPET 2. *Turns to* NARRATOR.) . . . Would you excuse me for a moment?

NARRATOR: Certainly.

PUPPET 1 *(moving to* PUPPET 2): Pardon me. Who are you?

PUPPET 2 *(to audience):* Oh, brother. What a cracked egg. *(To* PUPPET 1) I'm Santy Claus. Ho, ho, ho, ho.

PUPPET 1 *(bowing):* Pleased to meet you, Santa. *(Moves back to* NARRATOR)

NARRATOR *(to* PUPPET 1): You don't really think he's Santa Claus, do you?

PUPPET 1: No, but I'm not about to argue.

PUPPET 2 *(moving to* PUPPET 1): Hey, you. This is a stickup!

PUPPET 1: I was afraid he'd change the subject. *(To* PUPPET 2) Do you mind if I say one thing?

PUPPET 2: What's that?

PUPPET 1 *(screaming):* HELP!

(PUPPETS *exit to the sounds of crashes, screams, and thumps. When noise has stopped* PUPPET 2 *enters.)*

PUPPET 2: What a washout. Nothing but dumb, old hockey pucks. I better move on and see if I can find another mark.

NARRATOR: So poor Herman was beat up and left on the side of the road for dead.

(Enter PUPPET 1.)

PUPPET 1: Oh, the pain of it all! Pain! Pain!

NARRATOR: Although I can't see how anybody who makes that much noise can be thought to be dead.

PUPPET 1: Cool it. This is the dramatic part of the skit. Oh, pain!

NARRATOR: Don't hold your breath waiting for an Emmy. Anyway, there he lay, until someone started down the road toward him. It was a preacher from one of the churches in Herman's hometown.

(Enter PUPPET 3.)

PUPPET 1 *(loudly):* Oh, pain! Oh, help!

PUPPET 3 *(in a preaching voice):* I say to you, what a miserable sight. Can you believe it, brothers and sisters, that this poor soul has been beaten up by thieves and robbers. *(Looking up to heaven with a cry)* Can God help this poor soul?!? I say, YES! Do I hear an "A-MEN"?!?! *(Lowers voice and heads offstage)* Good preaching, brother. Yes, sir. That will make a fine sermon this Sunday.

(Exit PUPPET 3.*)*

PUPPET 1: Hey, wait a minute! Where are you going? This poor soul needs your help!

NARRATOR: But the preacher just walked on. Poor Herman just lay there getting worse.

PUPPET 1 *(not as loudly):* Oh, pain! Oh, agony!

NARRATOR: But, wait. Here comes another person down the road. Why, it's a member of the board at Herman's church.

(Enter PUPPET 4.*)*

PUPPET 1 *(loudly again):* Pain! Hurt! Major injuries!

PUPPET 4 *(stopping and nodding):* Dear me. What a simply filthy creature. Hmmm. He does look familiar. I really should do something to help him.

PUPPET 1: Now you're talkin', brother!

PUPPET 4: Why of course, I'll do something. I'll call together the finance committee and we can take a collection . . . no, wait . . . maybe it should be the education committee so we could organize a seminar . . . *(moves offstage)* . . . no, it should be the facilities committee, we could start a shelter . . . no, maybe the worship committee for prayer . . .

(Exit PUPPET 4.*)*

PUPPET 1: Wait a minute! How about a committee of one to help me right now?

NARRATOR: But the church board member went right on.

PUPPET 1: Man, nobody will stop and help me.

NARRATOR: Yes, the sun was setting, and Herman had just about given up hope, when down the road came another figure.

PUPPET 1: Who is it this time?

NARRATOR: Why it looks like a Samarimonster.

PUPPET 1: A Samarimonster? Oh, no. They're considered the lowest things on the earth. I don't even go near their towns. He'll never stop and help me.

NARRATOR: Well, here he comes anyway.

(Enter MONSTER.*)*

PUPPET 1 *(with no effort or feeling):* Oh, pain-agony-pain.

MONSTER: My goodness! You look awful!

PUPPET 1: Thanks loads. You don't look too great yourself!

MONSTER: What happen to you?

PUPPET 1 *(sarcastic):* I got stepped on by a giraffe. What do you think? I got mugged! Can't you tell?

MONSTER: Mugged by giraffe?

PUPPET 1: No, you idiot! I simply got mugged. Just forget it and leave me alone, like the others. Let me suffer in peace.

MONSTER: You not want Monster to help you?

PUPPET 1: Help? You mean you'd help me?

MONSTER: Sure!

PUPPET 1: But, why? You don't know me. In fact, I haven't even been very nice to you.

MONSTER: Well, you have bad day. If Monster was hurt, me would want help.

PUPPET 1: I don't know what to say.

MONSTER: Me take you to hospital now. Monster even take care of bill. Uh, what all these little, black, round things on road?

PUPPET 1: Those are hockey pucks. I sell them.

MONSTER *(picks one up and eats it):* Good stuff. Crunchy.

PUPPET 1: You're not supposed to eat . . .

MONSTER: Monster take 12 cases of hockey pucks.

PUPPET 1: Sold.

(Exit PUPPETS.)

NARRATOR: So, Herman learned a valuable lesson about who his real neighbors and friends were and how we should treat each other.

Focus Questions:

1. What happened to Herman on his way to Jericho?
2. Why, do you think, didn't the first two people stop and help Herman?
3. Why didn't Herman think the Samarimonster would help him?
4. Jesus asked, "Which of the people was a [good] neighbor to the man?" How would you answer that question?
5. What do you think Jesus meant when He said, "Love thy neighbor as thyself"?

The Prodigal Puppet

Biblical Text: Luke 15:10-32; Matthew 7:11

Scene Preparation: Read Luke 15:10. Then ask the children the following questions:
"How many of you have been punished by your parents?"
"How many of you have wanted to run away from home at some time?"
"What stopped you from running away?"
"Are you glad you didn't run away, or someone brought you back?"
NARRATOR will need cue cards printed with "Hooray" and "Boo."

Cast: NARRATOR, PUPPET 1, PUPPET 2, and PUPPET 3

NARRATOR: Before we start, we want you to know that you are going to be part of the story. We want you to be the party in the story. Here are your two cue cards. *(Show the audience "Hooray!" and "Boo.")* When we show you these cards, we need to hear you say them. Let's try it. *(Hold up each card for an audience response.)* Good. I think we can now begin our story. Once upon a time there lived a very wealthy man.

(Enter PUPPET 1.)

PUPPET 1: Tah-dah!

NARRATOR: This very wealthy man had two sons.

(Enter PUPPET 2 and PUPPET 3.)

PUPPET 2 and PUPPET 3: Tah-dah!

NARRATOR: These were two, fine, strong, loyal, wise. . . .

PUPPET 2 *(slapping PUPPET 1 on the back):* Hi-ya, Poppy!

NARRATOR *(pause):* Well, at least one fine, loyal, wise. . . .

PUPPET 3 *(slapping PUPPET 1 on the back)* Whatcha say, Daddy-o?

PUPPET 1 *(to NARRATOR):* Why don't we skip that part and move right along?

NARRATOR: Right. These two sons were very different.

PUPPET 2: Right-o! I'm exciting, fun-loving, coo-oo-ool, and vibra . . . uh . . . veeber . . . duh . . . viberating!

PUPPET 1: I think you vibrated a screw loose.

PUPPET 3: On the other hand, I'm hardworking and rugged, along with being suave and sophisticated.

PUPPET 1: Don't look now, Mr. Sophisticated, but you put your pants on backwards again today.

PUPPET 3: Oops.

(Exit PUPPET 3.)

NARRATOR: These boys were different in other ways also. Even though both of them were a little stubborn. One difference we can show you is when their father would ask the first son . . .

PUPPET 1 *(to* PUPPET 2): First son, I want you to go out into the east 40 and help the hired hands put up a fence.

NARRATOR: The first son would say . . .

PUPPET 2: Duh . . . right, Poppy!

(Exit PUPPET 1.)

NARRATOR: But later on . . .

PUPPET 2: Now what was I supposed to do? I can't seem to remember, so I guess I'll go to town and have some fun.

(Exit PUPPET 2. *Enter* PUPPET 1 *and* PUPPET 3.)

NARRATOR: Then the father would come to the other son. . . .

PUPPET 1: Other son, I want you to go out into the east 40 and help the hired hands put up a fence.

NARRATOR: This son would say . . .

PUPPET 3: No way, Daddy-o. I can't do it. I've got other plans.

(Exit PUPPET 1.)

NARRATOR: But later on . . .

PUPPET 3: I shouldn't have said that to Dad. I better do what he asked me. I'll head over to the east 40 and help with that fence.

(Exit PUPPET 3. *Enter* PUPPET 1.)

PUPPET 1: I like it a lot more when the one son said, "Forget it" and then changed his mind, than when the first son said he'd do it and then forgot.

(Enter PUPPET 2.)

NARRATOR: I think you can see that the first son really wasn't very bright.

PUPPET 2 *(to* NARRATOR): Hey, watch it!

NARRATOR: But he knew that he wanted to have fun, not work on his dad's ranch.

PUPPET 2: Hey, Poppy!

PUPPET 1: What is it?

PUPPET 2: I want to have some fun. I want to party! I need some money.

PUPPET 1: Well, you have a nice allowance.

PUPPET 2: I want more.

PUPPET 1: I pay you for your work.

PUPPET 2: I want more.

PUPPET 1: When I retire you'll get half of everything I own.

PUPPET 2: But I don't want to wait that long. I want my money now! Now, now, now, now, NOW!

PUPPET 1 *(to audience):* He takes after his mother's side of the family. *(To* PUPPET 2) I guess you're old enough to learn a lesson. I'll give you your share of my money.

PUPPET 2: Oh, goody, goody. *(Chanting)* Get down and par-ty. Par-ty. Par-ty. Par-ty.

(Exit PUPPETS.)

NARRATOR: So the son took his father's money and left home.

PUPPET 2: I'm never going to have to come back to this dump again. I'm loaded!

NARRATOR: He went all over the world. . . .

PUPPET 2: Monty Car-low.

NARRATOR: And everywhere he went he spent his money wildly.

PUPPET 2: Hey, everyone, let's PARTY!

AUDIENCE (NARRATOR *holds up cue card):* Hooray!

PUPPET 2: Al-co-pull-key. PARTY!

AUDIENCE (NARRATOR *holds up cue card):* Hooray!

PUPPET 2: Ree-o Day Jan-air-ee-oo. PARTY!

AUDIENCE (NARRATOR *holds up cue card):* Hooray!

PUPPET 2: Holly-wood. This is great! I'm going to party until . . . until . . .

NARRATOR: . . . Until he ran out of money.

AUDIENCE (NARRATOR *holds up cue card):* Boo!

PUPPET 2 *(to* NARRATOR): What did you say?

NARRATOR: You ran out of money.

AUDIENCE (NARRATOR *holds up cue card):* Boo!

PUPPET 2: Oh, oh. *(To audience)* Can anybody lend me a few bucks?

AUDIENCE (NARRATOR *holds up cue card):* BOO!

NARRATOR: All of his friends left him.

PUPPET 2: I'm lonely.

NARRATOR: To pay his bills, he had to sell everything he had, even his clothes.

PUPPET 2: I'm cold.

NARRATOR: He didn't have any money to buy food.

PUPPET 2: I'm hungry.

NARRATOR: And he couldn't find a job.

PUPPET 2: I'm really hungry.

NARRATOR: Finally, a small farmer let him take care of the pigs at his farm. But he couldn't pay any money, and the only food he could give the boy was the slop he fed the hogs. *(Pig grunts from backstage)*

PUPPET 2 *(to backstage):* Lighten up, Porky. You'll get your share when I'm done.

NARRATOR: Then one day he had a brilliant idea! Well, for him it was brilliant.

PUPPET 2: I have a brilliant idea. Even the lowest servants on my dad's ranch are 20 times better off than I am. Maybe I can beg a job off Dad. After all, I do know the farm. Why didn't I think of this sooner?

(Exit PUPPET 2.)

NARRATOR: I refuse to answer that. Anyway, the boy went home, only expecting to have a chance at being a servant. But at home . . .

(Enter PUPPET 1 *facing stage left.)*

PUPPET 1: Every day I come here looking for my lost son. Someday he will come. *(Enter* PUPPET 2 *from stage right.)* When he comes I will see him. Then I'll run to him. I'll hug him. I'll kiss him. I'll . . .

PUPPET 2 *(tapping* PUPPET 1 *on the shoulder):* Hi, Poppy.

PUPPET 1 *(startled):* Aaahh! I'll scream.

PUPPET 2: I have returned, Father.

PUPPET 1: My son, my son.

PUPPET 2: No, Father, I only want to be a servant.

PUPPET 1: My boy has returned.

PUPPET 2: Dad, I was dumb. I don't deserve to be your son.

PUPPET 1: You will always be my beloved son.

PUPPET 2: Will you listen to me, Dad? I should only be a servant!

PUPPET 1: OK. If you say so.

PUPPET 2 *(pause):* Well . . . I'm not inflexible about it.

PUPPET 1: Good. *(Hugging* PUPPET 2*)* Kill the fatted calf! Break out the finest food! Strike up the band! He's back!

PUPPET 2 *(softly):* Don't get me wrong, Poppy, but aren't we getting just a little carried away?

PUPPET 1 *(aside):* Don't cramp my style. This is my big scene. *(Loudly)* Oh, the lost has been found. *(Aside)* Where do we exit?

PUPPET 2: Stage right.

PUPPET 1: Was I good?

PUPPET 2: Just fine, Poppy, but don't expect an Oscar.

(Exit PUPPETS.*)*

NARRATOR: So the happy father threw a big party for his returned son. The party was in full swing when the other son arrived home from working in the fields.

(Enter PUPPET 1 *and* PUPPET 3.*)*

PUPPET 1: Oh rejoice! My lost son has returned!

PUPPET 3: Hey, Daddy-o! Mellow out! What's happening?

PUPPET 1: This is a great day! Your brother has returned!

PUPPET 3: That deadbeat? You mean this party is for him?

PUPPET 1: Yes. Isn't it marvelous?

PUPPET 3: No! It stinks. He runs off, breaks your heart, loses half your money, and then gets the royal treatment when he comes home. I stay here and work, and I can't even have my friends over for a pizza party.

PUPPET 1: Look, Son. Everything I have is yours. I love you. But today your brother, who was as good as dead, is back with us alive.

PUPPET 3: I think I can fix that!

PUPPET 1: Be happy with me, Son. Don't spoil this special day.

PUPPET 3: Well . . . OK. I'll do it for you, Dad.

(Exit PUPPETS.)

NARRATOR: God is like the father waiting for us to come home. Once we're home, there is great rejoicing. When others come home, let's be happy and rejoice with God.

Focus Questions:
1. Which boy do you think was the better son? Why?
2. What did the first son want?
3. What happened to the first boy when he left home?
4. What did he want to be when he came back home?
5. How did his father greet him when he came home?
6. How did his brother feel when he came home?
7. How is God like the father?
8. How are you like the son?

Cookies

Biblical Text: Matthew 25:14-30; 1 Corinthians 3:8; 1 Peter 4:10

Scene Preparation: On a chalkboard or a large piece of paper, list some things the children tell you that they do well or enjoy doing.

Cast: NARRATOR, PUPPET 1, PUPPET 2, PUPPET 3, and PUPPET 4

NARRATOR: Do you remember what we call the stories Jesus told? *(Wait for response)* That's right, parables. Well, today, we're going to hear another parable that Jesus told, slightly changed, but the message is the same. It starts off in a faraway land. In this faraway land there lived a very rich person . . .

(Enter PUPPET 1.*)*

PUPPET 1: John D. Rockacookie, at your service, but you can call me J. D.

NARRATOR: J. D. was perhaps the wealthiest person in the world.

PUPPET 1: That's right.

NARRATOR: He could buy anything he wanted.

PUPPET 1: Sure! Cars, yachts, mink-lined cookie jars, anything.

NARRATOR: And J. D. liked to travel to exotic countries.

PUPPET 1: I love it! I've been to the Great Wall of Cookies, the Pyramid of King Cookie II, and to the Baskin Robbins in Cookiemunga.

NARRATOR: Whenever J. D. went away on one of his trips, he left his many businesses in the charge of his trusted servants. That is what we're going to talk about right now. One day, J. D. was thinking, which was very hard work for him, and decided . . .

PUPPET 1: I think I want to go someplace new and exotic. I've got it! I'm going to visit the Black Hole of Cookiecutta! What a great idea! Boy, this thinking is hard work.

NARRATOR: So, J. D. packed his bags and made plans for his trip.

PUPPET 1: Let's see, do I have everything? Twelve packages of Oreos, 10 packages of Chips Ahoys, and 20 cases of animal crackers. That ought to hold me until tomorrow.

NARRATOR: Then he called in some of his trusted servants, three to be exact. He talked to them one by one. His most trusted servant was first.

(Enter PUPPET 2.)

PUPPET 2: You called, J. D.?

PUPPET 1: That's right. I've been thinking . . .

PUPPET 2: Oh, oh.

PUPPET 1: And I've decided to take a trip.

PUPPET 2: Oh, thrill.

PUPPET 1: I'm going to leave part of my business in your control.

PUPPET 2: You can count on me, J. D.

PUPPET 1: I know that. That's why I'm leaving you in charge of so much.

PUPPET 2: Exactly what am I going to have, J. D.?

PUPPET 1: I'm leaving you with . . . 5 million gingersnaps.

PUPPET 2: Wow! 5 million . . . *(puzzled)* . . . gingersnaps?

PUPPET 1: That's right. I want you to buy and sell with them . . .

PUPPET 2: Gingersnaps?

PUPPET 1: . . . And increase the value of what I'm leaving you.

PUPPET 2: Buy and sell with gingersnaps?

PUPPET 1: And if you do well, I will reward you when I return.

PUPPET 2: Right, J. D. *(Exiting)* What do you do with 5 million gingersnaps?

NARRATOR: So the first servant left, a little confused, but determined to do his best with what he was given.

PUPPET 2 *(from offstage):* Gingersnaps?

NARRATOR: In came the next servant. *(Enter* PUPPET 3.) He was also a very good worker and almost as trusted as the first servant.

PUPPET 3: You rang, J. D.?

PUPPET 1: Yes, second trusted servant. I am going on a long trip, so I am going to leave part of my vast business empire in your keeping.

PUPPET 3: Totally awesome, J. D.

PUPPET 1 *(to audience):* Some of my servants are a little strange. *(To* PUPPET 3) I have decided to leave you 2 million Vienna Fingers.

PUPPET 3: Like, far out, J. D. You can count on . . . 2 million what?

PUPPET 1: I want you to trade and sell these Vienna Fingers like they were your own . . .

PUPPET 3: Vienna Fingers? Trade and sell?

PUPPET 1: . . . And increase the value of what I'm leaving you. . . .

PUPPET 2: And he called me strange?

PUPPET 1: . . . And if you do well, I will reward you when I return.

PUPPET 2: Sure thing, J. D. *(Exiting)* The old man's finally lost it.

NARRATOR: So our second servant left J. D. Rockacookie, just as confused, but just as determined as the first servant to make a good showing and prove himself. Finally, in came the third servant. *(Enter* PUPPET 4.) I'm not even going to try and describe him. You'll get the idea.

PUPPET 4: Duh . . . I heard you called for me, uh, J. D., and so here I am, yup, yup, yup, yup.

PUPPET 1: Very good. I'm going on a long trip.

PUPPET 4: Wow! Neato! Uh, bone voyagie!

PUPPET 1: Thank you, I think. I am going to leave you part of my business to handle.

PUPPET 4: Oh, boy *(chanting),* I get to be the boss. I get to be the boss. I get to be the . . .

PUPPET 1: Excuse me. May I finish?

PUPPET 4: Why, sure.

PUPPET 1: While I'm gone I want you to make a profit on my business. If you do, I'll reward you when I come back.

PUPPET 4: Oh, goodie! Can I have a Mickey Mouse hat?

PUPPET 1: Just handle my business while I'm gone.

PUPPET 4: Whatcha gonna give me?

PUPPET 1: I want you to use 1 million macaroons.

PUPPET 4: Wow-wee! That's a lot of macaroons. Yup, yup, yup, yup.

PUPPET 1: Do you think you can handle it?

PUPPET 4: Why, sure, boss. You can count on me.

PUPPET 1: I hope so. Well, I'll see you later.

(Exit PUPPET 1.)

PUPPET 4: Wow! One million macaroons! Boy, that sure is a bunch. . . . I wonder what a macaroon is, anyway?

NARRATOR: So J. D. Rockacookie went on his way, and his three servants started working, or rather the first two did. The third servant was lazy and a little *(glance at* PUPPET 4 *and then whisper to the audience)* D-U-M-B. So he thought up a plan.

PUPPET 4: And a great plan it is too. Yup, yup, yup, yup.

NARRATOR: Really? What are you going to do?

PUPPET 4: I'm going to bury them.

NARRATOR: Bury 1 million macaroon cookies?

PUPPET 4: Yup, yup, yup, yup. Is that what macaroons are?

NARRATOR *(to audience):* Is that what J. D. Rockacookie wanted this servant to do? Of course not! He wanted him to use those cookies and work with them.

PUPPET 4: Nope, nope, nope, nope. I couldn't do that. Too dangerous. I might lose them or something. Then J. D. would be mad at me.

(Exit PUPPET 4.)

NARRATOR: Well, after a long time, J. D. Rockacookie returned from his journey.

(Enter PUPPET 1.)

PUPPET 1: What a great trip! But now, I'm a little hungry. I think I'll call in my three trusted servants.

NARRATOR: And that's exactly what J. D. did, starting with his most trusted servant.

PUPPET 1: Number one, come on down!

(Enter PUPPET 2.)

PUPPET 2: Here I am, J. D. Did you have a nice trip?

PUPPET 1: Yes, but I'm hungry. What happened to my 5 million gingersnaps?

PUPPET 2: Well, I did what you said and traded and sold them, until now, I can give you back 10 million chocolate chip cookies!

PUPPET 1: Ten million! Fantastic! That's great! I'm giving you a big raise and putting you in charge of all my cookie factories. You are now a vice president in my company!

PUPPET 2: Thanks a lot, J. D. What do you want me to do with all the cookies?

PUPPET 1: Have them shipped to my house. I'll get to them . . . soon.

(Exit PUPPET 2.)

NARRATOR: Then it was time for the second servant.

PUPPET 1: Number two, where are you?

(Enter PUPPET 3.)

PUPPET 3: Here I am, J. D. I hope you had a radical trip.

PUPPET 1: Thank you, I did . . . I think. What happened to my 2 million Vienna Fingers?

PUPPET 3: Well, I did what you said and traded and sold them, until now I can give you back 4 million double-stuffed Oreos!

PUPPET 1: Four million! Awesome! Totally radical! I'm giving you a big raise and putting in charge of all cookie sales. You are now a vice president in my company!

PUPPET 3: Far out! Thanks, J. D.!

(Exit PUPPET 3.)

NARRATOR: Finally J. D. came to the final servant.

PUPPET 1: Number three, sign in please!

PUPPET 4: Yup, yup, yup, yup. Here I am, boss.

PUPPET 1: What do you have to show me after using my 1 million macaroons for all this time?

PUPPET 4: You're gonna be so proud of me, boss. I was real careful, 'cause I knew you liked cookies . . .

PUPPET 1: Fine, but what did you . . .

PUPPET 4: . . . And I knew you'd be mad if I lost them. . . .

PUPPET 1: Just tell me what you . . .

PUPPET 4: So I used my head, like my ma always . . .

PUPPET 1 *(frustrated):* WHERE ARE MY COOKIES!?!

PUPPET 4: Uh, right outside your office window, boss.

PUPPET 1 *(looking behind him):* Why, those are the same macaroons I gave you, I think. They're all dirty and muddy.

PUPPET 4: Yup, yup, yup, yup. I buried them so nobody could take them.

PUPPET 1 *(yelling):* You buried them! You ruined my cookies! You're fired! I'll see that you never work for anyone again! Get out of here and never come back!

PUPPET 4 *(flustered):* R-r-r-right, boss, I mean, J. D., I mean ex-boss.

PUPPET 1: OUT!

(Exit PUPPETS.*)*

NARRATOR: You see, God gives us things to work with down here on earth. We call them skills or talents. Just like each servant, we are to use them wisely. If we do, then our skills and talents will increase, and God will give us even more rewards. But if we don't use our talents and skills, they can be taken away from us. Let's use our talents for God.

Focus Questions:

1. What did the first two servants receive for doing a good job?
2. What did the third servant do with his cookies? Why?
3. Why do you think the rich man gave his servants different amounts of cookies?
4. What happened to the third servant?
5. What do you think will happen if you use your talents well?
6. What do you think will happen if you don't use your talents?

Peter Escapes

Biblical Text: Acts 12:1-19; Romans 8:31

Scene Preparation: Ask the children the following questions:
"Can you think of any dangerous situation that scared you so much, that you were sure you wouldn't survive?"
"Did it feel like a miracle when everything was done?"
"What did you do?" or "What would you do if it happened to you?"

Cast: NARRATOR, PUPPET 1, and PUPPET 2 *(to be fitted with wings)*

NARRATOR: We're going to tell you about one of the most unusual prison escapes ever. Do you know who did it?

(Enter PUPPET 1.)

PUPPET 1: The Bird Man of Alcatraz.

NARRATOR: No, this is a Bible story.

PUPPET 1: Great! I love Bible stories. Can I help?

NARRATOR: Sure. Is there anyone else back there who would like to help?

(Enter PUPPET 2.)

PUPPET 2: Well . . . I . . . uh . . . just happen to be passing along here, so if you need help, I am here to save the day!

PUPPET 1: Big deal.

NARRATOR: All right. *(Designating* PUPPET 1) You are going to play the part of Peter.

PUPPET 1 *(with pride):* Naturally you would pick me to be Peter. That strong, brave man from the Bible. Who else to play . . .

PUPPET 2: Oh, pleeeease! Give me a break.

NARRATOR *(designating* PUPPET 2): Now you head offstage and get into costume. Your part is very important.

PUPPET 2: Naturally.

NARRATOR: Let me set the scene for our story.

PUPPET 1: No! No! Let me!

NARRATOR: I don't know. . . .

PUPPET 1: Listen. *(Melodramatically)* It was a dark, windy night. . . .

NARRATOR: That's all right. . . .

PUPPET 1: . . . The dark, gothic house casts a shadow over the countryside. . . .

NARRATOR: Dark, gothic house? . . .

PUPPET 1: . . . A shot rings out in the darkness . . .

NARRATOR: Wait a minute, here!

PUPPET 1: A scream is heard. AAAAAHHHH! (PUPPET 1 *drops backstage.*)

NARRATOR *(losing patience):* Now cut that out! (PUPPET 1 *reenters.*)

PUPPET 1: Pretty good, huh?

NARRATOR: Well. . . .

PUPPET 2 *(voice offstage):* It stunk!

NARRATOR: Why not listen for a moment. This story starts in the city of Jerusalem long, long, ago. . . .

PUPPET 1 *(in low voice):* . . . In a galaxy far, far away.

NARRATOR: Maybe I need another Peter.

PUPPET 1: I'll be good.

NARRATOR: All right. Peter had been preaching with James, the brother of John. . . .

PUPPET 1 *(loudly):* All right, you dirty rotten sinners . . . REPENT!

NARRATOR *(trying to ignore the interruption):* . . . Thousands of people had joined the church, and thousands more wanted to come hear Peter.

PUPPET 1 *(to* PUPPET 2 *offstage):* You hear that? I'm a star!

NARRATOR: Everybody was happy. . . .

PUPPET 1: Yeah!

NARRATOR: . . . Almost. . . .

PUPPET 1: Oops.

NARRATOR: Peter and James had made some very powerful people angry.

PUPPET 1: Sorry.

NARRATOR: They had told Peter and James to stop preaching. But Peter and James wouldn't stop.

PUPPET 2 *(from offstage):* Just can't stop talking, can you?

NARRATOR: So they arrested Peter and James again and decided that they needed to punish them.

PUPPET 1 *(a little scared):* Punish?

NARRATOR: These people convinced King Herod to kill James. . . .

PUPPET 1 *(swallowing hard):* Gulp! Kill?

NARRATOR: When King Herod saw that this made these very important people very happy, he decided to kill Peter too.

PUPPET 1 *(scared):* KILL?!?! *(Offstage to* PUPPET 2*)* Hey! You want to switch parts? I don't think I want to be Peter anymore!

PUPPET 2 *(from offstage):* No way! You wanted it. You got it!

NARRATOR: So King Herod siezed Peter and threw him into prison. *(Grabs and "throws"* PUPPET 1 *back stage.* PUPPET 1 *screams, and a crash is heard backstage.)* Peter was placed in the deepest, darkest dungeon behind many closed and locked doors. They put their strongest chains on him. They had their roughest guards watch him. *(Enter* PUPPET 1.*)*

PUPPET 1: Aren't they going a little overboard for little ol' me?

NARRATOR: But in spite of this, do you think Peter was afraid? Do you think he was discouraged?

PUPPET 1: Yes!

NARRATOR: No.

PUPPET 1: No?

NARRATOR: Peter was ready for whatever was going to happen. He trusted Jesus to either save him or take him to heaven.

PUPPET 1: Wow, Peter really was brave.

NARRATOR: Peter refused to worry. In fact, he was so calm, he went to sleep.

PUPPET 1: Who can sleep! I'm too excited!

NARRATOR: Just go to sleep.

PUPPET 1: I don't think I can.

NARRATOR *(pushing* PUPPET 1*'s head down):* SLEEP!

PUPPET 1: Right. *(Snores loudly and quickly. Then slows and gets quieter.)*

NARRATOR *(to* PUPPET 2 *offstage):* OK. Now it's your turn.

PUPPET 2 *(from offstage):* I don't know about this.

NARRATOR: Come on. You'll be great! *(Enter* PUPPET 2 *with wings on.)*

PUPPET 2: You didn't tell me I was going to be a bird.

NARRATOR: You're not a bird. You're an angel.

PUPPET 2: An angel? What do I do?

NARRATOR: You lead Peter out of prison.

PUPPET 2: But what about the guards and the chains and the locks?

NARRATOR: God takes care of those, like magic.

PUPPET 2: Hey, that's cool! Uh . . . what do I do now?

NARRATOR: Well, if you're going to lead Peter out of prison, you'd better wake him up first.

PUPPET 2: Good idea. *(Moving to* PUPPET 1) Hey, Peter. (PUPPET 1 *keeps snoring.* PUPPET 2 *shakes him a little bit.)* Wake up, Peter! (PUPPET 1 *keeps snoring.* PUPPET 2 *yells.)* Yo! Peter! Move it, Buster!

PUPPET 1 *(jerking awake):* Whaaa!

PUPPET 2: Come on, Peter, it's time to go.

PUPPET 1: Who are you?

PUPPET 2: I'm an angel.

PUPPET 1 *(pause):* Naw! You can't be an angel.

PUPPET 2: Sure I am! *(Turning)* Look at my wings.

PUPPET 1: How do I know you're not just a big dodo bird, or something.

PUPPET 2 *(deep breath):* Listen. Do you want out of here, or do you want King Herod's archers to make you look like a porcupine tomorrow?

PUPPET 1 *(in deep voice, a.k.a. Tonto):* Anything you say, Kemosabe.

PUPPET 2: That's better. Just follow me.

PUPPET 1 *(to* NARRATOR): Is this for real? Was Peter able to just walk out of the prison?

NARRATOR: When the angel woke him up, Peter's chains were gone, he couldn't see a single guard, and all the prison doors were wide open.

PUPPET 2: Shall we go? *(Exit* PUPPET 2.)

PUPPET 1: Feet, don't fail me now. *(Exit* PUPPET 1.)

NARRATOR: So Peter followed the angel right out of the prison and right on home. In the morning, King Herod found the doors closed tight, the guards in place, the chains still locked, but no Peter. You see, as the Bible says, "If God is for us, who can be against us?" King Herod found out the hard way.

Focus Questions:
1. Who was the king that was in our story?
2. What were Peter and James doing that people didn't like?
3. How do you think Peter felt when he was in prison?
4. Do you think Peter would start preaching again?
5. What would you say to King Herod if you were one of the guards?

Christmas Offering

A Simple Christmas Program for
Children's Choir, Soloists, and Three Puppets

Cast: NARRATOR, PUPPET 1, PUPPET 2, PUPPET 3

(Enter PUPPET 1.)

PUPPET 1: Welcome, ladies and gentlemen, boys and girls, and all creatures great and small. We are here today to celebrate the most wonderful day of the year, *Christmas!*

(CHILDREN *run to choir places. Enter* PUPPET 2 *and* PUPPET 3.)

CHILDREN, PUPPET 2, and PUPPET 3: Whoopee! Hooray! Yeah! Etc.

PUPPET 1: Christmas is a time when we remember . . .

PUPPET 2: Candy!

PUPPET 3: Presents!

PUPPET 2: Turkey!

PUPPET 3 *(louder):* Presents!

PUPPET 2: Christmas trees!

PUPPET 3 *(louder still):* Presents!

PUPPET 2: Presents!

PUPPET 3 *(loudest):* PRESENTS!

PUPPET 2: Hey, I already said that.

PUPPET 3: Oh, sorry.

PUPPET 1: Wait a minute. Those aren't the things we should remember on Christmas. Come on. What's the whole reason behind Christmas?

PUPPET 2: Oh, that's easy.

PUPPET 1: Good. What is it?

PUPPET 2 *and* PUPPET 3 *(look at each other and say together):* PRESENTS!

PUPPET 1 *(puts head down):* I don't think I'm going to make it. *(To* PUPPET 2 *and* PUPPET 3) Look, people, we're going to sing some songs. These Christmas carols might ring a bell and help you remember what Christmas means.

PUPPET 3: Ring a bell? Oh! Yup, yup, yup, yup.

PUPPET 2: Yeah. I get it, now.

(CHILDREN *sing chorus of "Jingle Bells" with* PUPPET 2 *and* PUPPET 3 *joining in on "HEY!")*

PUPPET 1: I don't think you quite understand. Maybe this carol will show you what I mean.

(Exit PUPPETS.)

(CHILDREN *sing first verse of "O Come, All Ye Faithful.")*

(Enter PUPPETS.)

PUPPET 3: Who's this "Christ the Lord"?

PUPPET 1: That's Jesus. He was born on Christmas.

PUPPET 2: Bummer.

PUPPET 1: What?

PUPPET 2: That poor guy only got one set of presents for birthday and Christmas.

PUPPET 3: Yup, yup, yup, yup. Only one set of presents.

PUPPET 1: You guys have one-track minds.

PUPPET 3: Wow! I'm smarter than I thought.

PUPPET 1: OK. You're right. Christmas is a time for gifts.

PUPPET 2 and PUPPET 3 *(congratulating each other):* All right!

PUPPET 1: But do you know why we give gifts?

PUPPET 3: Because Santy Claus is making a list and checking it twice. He's . . .

PUPPET 2 *(bumping* PUPPET 3): Cut it out! *(To* PUPPET 1) I really never thought of it.

PUPPET 1: The greatest gift ever given was God giving His Son, Jesus, to us on that very first Christmas. He was the first Christmas gift.

PUPPET 3: Was He wrapped in pretty paper?

PUPPET 1: They didn't wrap Him in paper. He was wrapped in a cloth by His mother, Mary.

PUPPET 3: Then she put Him under a Christmas tree?

PUPPET 1 *(shaking head):* No. In fact, He was laid in a manger. Listen to this.

(Exit PUPPETS.)

(CHILDREN *sing "Away in a Manger." Try all three verses. Good place for one or two soloists.)*

(Enter PUPPETS.)

PUPPET 1: Well?

PUPPET 3: I think my mind is still on the wrong track.

PUPPET 2: I think it's been derailed. It sounds like Jesus was a pretty special Guy.

PUPPET 1: He was. And He was born in a very special way. Let's try to picture that night.

PUPPET 2: I think I can picture it.

PUPPET 1: You can?

PUPPET 2: It was a dark, cold night . . .

PUPPET 1 *(nodding):* Very good.

PUPPET 2: . . . The moon peeks out from behind the clouds. . . .

PUPPET 1 *(nodding):* All right.

PUPPET 2: . . . A moon beam falls on the deserted mansion. . . .

PUPPET 1 *(stops nodding):* Say what?

PUPPET 2: . . . A pirate ship sails on the horizon. . . .

PUPPET 3 *(nodding):* This is good!

PUPPET 1: Now wait a minute!

PUPPET 2: . . . Suddenly, the lights go out. A scream is heard. . . .

PUPPET 3 *(frantic):* What is it!

PUPPET 2: I don't know!

PUPPET 1: IT'S THE WRONG SCENE! THAT'S WHAT IT IS!

PUPPET 2: Well, maybe I got carried away a little. But I bet there was a lot excitement and noise and celebrating on the night when Jesus was born.

PUPPET 1: Not really. Jesus was born on a quiet, still night.

(Exit PUPPETS.*)*

*(*CHILDREN *sing "Silent Night." Sing as many verses as you want. Another good spot for a soloist.)*

(Enter PUPPETS.*)*

PUPPET 3: Sounds too quiet. It must not have been very exciting.

PUPPET 2: Yeah. There should have been fireworks and parties and singing.

PUPPET 1: It was better than that and much more exciting. This was such a great day that angels came down from heaven and sang songs about it.

PUPPET 3: Wow! Real angels! That must have been real purty.

PUPPET 2: That is special. The only sound that was heard when I was born was screaming.

PUPPET 1: You cried a lot when you were born, huh?

PUPPET 2: No, but my doctor did. I bit him.

PUPPET 1: The sound shepherds heard on that night many years ago was the sweetest music you could imagine. Thousands of angels singing and shining brightly in the sky.

PUPPET 2: Sounds just a little scary to me. I've never seen an angel.

PUPPET 3: Neither have I.

PUPPET 1: Neither had the shepherds. And you're right. It was scary. But one of the angels told them, "Don't be afraid. We have great news for you and all mankind. Your Savior, the King of Kings, has just been born in Bethlehem."

PUPPET 2: And the shepherds believed them?

PUPPET 1: Wouldn't you?

PUPPET 3: Uh, yup, yup, yup, yup.

(Exit PUPPETS.*)*

*(*CHILDREN *sing "Angels We Have Heard on High.")*

(Enter PUPPETS.*)*

PUPPET 1: So the shepherds went and found Jesus in the manger.

PUPPET 3: Right! In a manger. Uh . . . what's a manger?

PUPPET 1: Well, it a . . . a . . . place where you put hay for animals to eat.

PUPPET 3: Oh . . . what?

PUPPET 2: Wait a minute. Just where was this manger?

PUPPET 1: In a barn in Bethlehem.

PUPPET 2: A barn! You said He was a king! He should have been in a castle!

PUPPET 3: Or at least a hospital.

PUPPET 1: No. Jesus was going to live on this earth as a poor person. That's why He was born in a place like a barn.

PUPPET 2: I still think He should have been born in a special place.

PUPPET 1: Jesus made that stable a special place.

(Exit PUPPETS.*)*

(CHILDREN *sing "What Child Is This?" You might have soloist on verses and choir come in on choruses.)*

(Enter PUPPETS.*)*

PUPPET 3: I still don't know why this means we get presents on Christmas.

PUPPET 1: You see, people came and worshiped Jesus and gave Him gifts on Christmas.

PUPPET 2: Big deal. A bunch of dirty shepherds come. What presents can they give, besides a dumb sheep?

PUPPET 1: Well . . .

PUPPET 3: Uh . . . white fleas.

PUPPET 1 and PUPPET 2 *(look at each other):* White fleas?

PUPPET 3: Yup, yup, yup, yup. Their little sheepies had "fleas" as white as snow.

(PUPPET 1 *and* PUPPET 2 *cover their eyes with their hands.)*

PUPPET 2 *(to* PUPPET 1): You were going to say?

PUPPET 1: Besides the shepherds, three wise men from the east followed a star that led them to Jesus. They also brought gifts to Jesus.

PUPPET 2: What were their gifts?

PUPPET 1: They brought some shiny gold . . .

PUPPET 2: Wow!

PUPPET 1: . . . Some sweet-smelling frankincense . . .

PUPPET 2: That's neat.

PUPPET 1: . . . And myrrh.

PUPPET 3: Is that anything like "white fleas"?

PUPPET 2: Shut up and sing.

(PUPPETS *sing "We Three Kings." Have fun with it. For instance, on the line "Westward leading . . ." all three puppets can point in different directions. Do the chorus twice, and on the second time* PUPPET 3 *can hold out the "O" for a long, long time until the other puppets stop him.*)

PUPPET 2: Wow, with all of this attention, I bet Jesus became someone really powerful and famous when He grew up.

PUPPET 1: Yes and no.

PUPPET 3: I think I just got derailed again.

PUPPET 1: Jesus did do many wonderful things, but a lot of people hated Him.

PUPPET 2: Did He become powerful?

PUPPET 1: Not the way you mean. Jesus did many miracles and helped a lot of people. But finally, they killed Him.

PUPPET 3 *(sniff):* I hate stories with sad endings.

PUPPET 1: But this story has a happy ending. Jesus was dead but for only three days. Then He came out of the grave, and today He is ready to love us. He's even building a place for us in heaven.

PUPPET 2: You mean, He wants us to live with Him?

PUPPET 1: That's right. I guess you can say we still haven't received God's final Christmas present. Jesus is coming back for us again. But even today, Jesus gives us gifts of love, peace, and joy.

(Exit PUPPETS.)

(CHILDREN *sing "Joy to the World."*)

(Enter PUPPETS. PUPPET 2 *and* PUPPET 3 *look sad.*)

PUPPET 1: Hey, what's wrong? I thought the Christmas story would make you happy?

PUPPET 2: It does.

PUPPET 3: Yup, yup, yup, yup. But . . .

PUPPET 1: But what?

PUPPET 2: We know about Jesus' big Christmas gift for us, but we haven't got anything for Him.

PUPPET 3: Yup, yup, yup. It's even His birthday, and all I have is 17 cents and an old skate key. I can't get anything good enough for Jesus.

PUPPET 1: That's nice. Jesus loves you and will accept whatever you can give, as long as you give it to Him with love. He wants to be your Friend.

PUPPET 2: I think it would be great to have Jesus as a friend.

PUPPET 3: Do you think He'd like 17 cents and a skate key?

PUPPET 1: Probably. Almost as much as "white fleas."

(PUPPETS *exit.*)

(CHILDREN *sing "O Come All Ye Faithful." Make sure to include the last verse.*)